PERSONALITY WORKBOOK

40 Character-Revealing Quizzes

Ben Tausig

FALL RIVER PRESS

A QUIRK PACKAGING BOOK

Design and illustrations by Tanya Ross-Hughes/Hotfoot Studio

Fall River Press
122 Fifth Avenue
New York, NY 10011

ISBN: 978-1-4351-2489-9

Printed and bound in the United States

10 9 8 7 6 5 4 3 2 1

To Ted Mallison, for whom "green lightning" could have been named.

The author would like to acknowledge Chris Barsanti at Fall River Press and Sharyn Rosart at Quirk Packaging for the opportunity to write this book, Erin Canning for her patient editing, and Tanya Ross-Hughes for her great design.

CONTENTS

Chapter 3: YOU + LIFESTYLE 69

Chapter 4: YOU + CAREER 99

Introduction

Through a playful combination of diagnostic quizzes and pop psychology, discover interesting information about your favorite subject—you!

Divided into four chapters, the 40 quizzes in *Personality Workbook* are fun to do, easy to score, and full of sage advice. Play with this book and find out just who you are—share with friends and family for a better understanding of those around you.*

HOW TO USE *PERSONALITY WORKBOOK*

Write your answers directly in this book or on a separate piece of paper. Unless noted otherwise, the multiple-choice questions only have one answer. You may find that more than one answer or none of the answers appeals to you, but for accurate Results, choose the most fitting answer—there are no right or wrong answers. Once you complete the quiz, add up your points using the Key. Then use your Total points to find out your Result! Keep reading to find out more about the areas of your life you'll be exploring.

You: Your style, originality, and emotional well-being are tested in this chapter.

You + Others: Your relationships with friends and romantic partners are assessed here.

You + Lifestyle: This chapter examines your social life, your home life, and your sense of adventure.

You + Career: Here you'll find insight about your current career, work habits, and interactions with coworkers.

*Please keep in mind that *Personality Workbook* is for personal entertainment only. The advice dispensed here should not replace the advice of a licensed professional.

Chapter 1: **YOU**

Are You an Original Thinker?

1. Your friend asks for a word that rhymes with "Sam." Quick! What's the first thing that comes to your head? _____

2. You're cooking, and the recipe calls for milk. But there's none in the fridge! What do you do? _____

3. What is art? _____

4. Your friend asks you to make up a three-word song title, where all the words rhyme. Quick! Can you think of something that makes sense in ten seconds? _____

   _____

5. Name a shape other than a square. _____

6. You're stuck in traffic. You a) turn on the radio b) honk c) think about other things

7. Pick a number between 1 and 10. _____

8. What do you do on a rainy day? a) Find an indoor activity b) Find something to do out in the rain c) Wait it out patiently

9. Name as many colors as you can that start with the letter "T" in ten seconds. _____

   _____

10. Green is the hot color in fashion this season. What color shirt do you want to buy? _____

Think about what items you would add to the following scenarios.

11. What kind of accessories might a person be wearing? _____

_____

12. What kind of things might you find in a fishbowl? _____

_____

13. What might you find in a frame hanging on a wall? _____

_____

14. What kind of things might be written on a chalkboard in a classroom? _____

_____

15. What kind of things might you find in a shopping cart? _____

_____

KEY

1. 1 point for an everyday three-letter word like YAM or JAM; 2 points for a word with four or more letters, like SCRAM; 3 points for an unusual word like LAM, or a nonsense word like XAM.

2. 1 point for running out to the store; 2 points for making a different dish; 3 points for substituting a different ingredient.

3. 1 point for something like "It hangs in a museum"; 2 points for something like "A sculpture or a painting"; 3 points for something like "A means of human expression."

4. 3 points for a successful title!

5. 1 point for another round shape or a three- or four-sided shape; 2 points for a shape with five or more sides; 3 points for a three-dimensional shape like a sphere or cube.

6. a) 2 b) 3 c) 1

7. 1 point for picking 7; 2 points for picking 1 or 10; 3 points for picking any other number.

8. a) 2 b) 3 c) 1

9. 1 point if you can't think of any; 2 points if you can think of one; 3 points if you can think of two or more.

10. 1 point if you buy a green shirt; 2 points if you buy a totally different color; 3 points if you buy a similar color like aqua.

11. 1 point for a hat or purse; 2 points for jewelry; 3 points for anything else

12. 1 point for a fish; 2 points for a fish plus rocks and figurines; 3 points for anything else

13. 1 point for a photo; 2 points for a painting; 3 points for anything else

14. 1 point for words; 2 points for a math problem; 3 points for anything else

15. 1 point for food items; 2 points for non-food items; 3 points for a child or something silly

Total ____

RESULTS

14–19 points
You think like STEPHEN HAWKING. You have a very rational mind and tend to think objectively. You evaluate situations carefully and attempt to respond in the most appropriate way possible. You draw heavily on past experiences.

20–26 points
You think like MOZART. You have a mostly rational mind, and you find orderliness very beautiful. You enjoy art most when it's not abstract and when every part of it fits together well.

27–32 points
You think like EINSTEIN. You have a cautiously creative mind, combining inventiveness with logic. You are capable of quick, on-the-spot mental work, but you remain grounded in concepts that make sense to you.

33–39 points
You think like SHAKESPEARE. You are creative—if there isn't a word for the thing you want to say, you're not afraid to make up a new one. You love stories of human drama, and you are drawn to poetry.

40–45 points
You think like DR. SEUSS. You are highly spontaneous and prone to energetic bursts of original thought. You deliberately attempt to avoid rehearsing tried-and-true patterns, and prefer to forge your own mental paths.

What Puzzle Type Challenges You Most?

Words

1. I find word definitions a) totally draining b) mostly dry
   c) fascinating

2. When solving problems, I a) take as long as I need to finish
   b) continue until I can't do anymore, then give up c) give up
   very quickly

3. Grammatical rules a) feel a little beyond me b) are simple and
   elegant c) are too intellectual

4. I read a) every day, usually the newspaper b) as much as I can
   get my hands on c) rarely, if ever

5. People who read a lot a) are interesting and well-rounded
   b) seem so smart! c) have too much time on their hands

Numbers

6. I find math a) dull b) fun, but easy to mess up c) a total blast

7. When crunching numbers of any kind, I a) am very careful
   b) race through as quickly as possible c) can't be bothered to
   try very hard at all

8. Mathematical rules are a) too complicated b) simple and elegant
   c) interesting, though I have a hard time remembering them

9. I work with numbers a) maybe once a day b) as often as I can
   c) rarely, if ever

10. People who are good at math a) are smart and focused
    b) are intriguing, but have a very different kind of mind from
    me c) are weird

Pictures

11. Photographs and paintings are a) not that interesting to me
    b) OK, I guess c) often fun and fascinating

12. When looking at pictures, I a) often look for a long time
    b) glance for as long as I'm interested c) can't be bothered
    to look for very long

13. Visual art is a) a snooze b) engaging c) OK, I guess

14. I look at pictures a) a couple times a day b) as often as
    possible c) very rarely

15. People who like visual art a) have too much time on their
    hands b) are open-minded c) enjoy a different kind of art
    from what I enjoy

KEY

Words	Numbers	Pictures
1. a) 1 b) 2 c) 3	**6.** a) 1 b) 2 c) 3	**11.** a) 1 b) 2 c) 3
2. a) 3 b) 2 c) 1	**7.** a) 3 b) 2 c) 1	**12.** a) 3 b) 2 c) 1
3. a) 2 b) 3 c) 1	**8.** a) 1 b) 3 c) 2	**13.** a) 1 b) 3 c) 2
4. a) 2 b) 3 c) 1	**9.** a) 2 b) 3 c) 1	**14.** a) 2 b) 3 c) 1
5. a) 3 b) 2 c) 1	**10.** a) 3 b) 2 c) 1	**15.** a) 1 b) 3 c) 2

Total _____   Total _____   Total _____

RESULTS

If you received the most points on the Words section, you are a CROSSWORD person. You are a good qualitative thinker who is able to manage large amounts of abstract information, including language and meaning, in a controlled fashion. You are comfortable with change and adapt well to new situations. You are playful.

If you received the most points on the Numbers section, you are a SUDOKU person. You are a good quantitative thinker, most comfortable in situations where there are definite answers to every question and where little is left to chance. You are capable of working through long and complex problems, as long as you are confident that there is a solution waiting at the end. You are skilled at picking out patterns.

If you received the most points on the Pictures section, you are a WORD SEARCH person. You are a visual learner and watch the world around you very strongly. You prefer objects you can touch, smell, and taste to intellectual abstractions. You have a no-nonsense personality, and you are skilled at identifying what's important.

If Words and Numbers were tied for the most points, you are a LOGIC puzzle person. You like figuring out problems that have very precise answers and that are solved by deduction rather than memory.

If Words and Pictures were tied for the most points, you are a TRIVIA person. You are a Renaissance man or woman—you read a lot about many different subjects. You enjoy being tested on subjects like world affairs and history.

If Numbers and Pictures were tied for the most points, you are a SPOT-THE-DIFFERENCE puzzle person. You enjoy focusing intently on things without having to think about them too intellectually. You are good at picking up on subtle differences.

Are You Right- or Left-Brained?

1. The best way to solve an argument is to a) let bygones be bygones b) work things out rationally c) let both sides have equal time to explain themselves

2. The best way for a city to deal with pollution is to a) tax the major sources b) educate people about how to pollute less c) attract greener industries

3. People worldwide would get along better if they a) took the time to understand one another better b) worried less about how others live c) lived more like me

4. When there is a limited amount of a necessary resource, the best way to deal with the problem is to a) figure out how to share what we have b) distribute an equal amount to everyone c) figure out how to increase the amount of the goods at the source

5. The point of education is to a) give children tools to succeed in the job market b) stimulate exciting new ideas in young minds c) give people good social environments from a young age

6. There is a long line at the bank. They should a) add more employees b) stay open a little longer, for goodness' sake c) ignore the customers when they ask silly questions!

7. A house should be organized a) in whatever way feels right over time b) in advance, with an eye toward making it as efficient as possible to get around c) in a way that makes you enjoy sitting in each room

8. Children should be raised a) according to their individual personalities b) according to predetermined methods c) with as much love as possible

9. The Internet is great for a) reading up on topics I know little or nothing about b) keeping in touch with friends c) finding up-to-the-minute information

10. When I shop, I a) linger as long as possible, checking out all the options b) get in and get out with exactly what I came for c) usually get distracted by things I didn't even come to the store for

11. The most beautiful gardens are a) planted in well-ordered rows b) full of wild surprises c) intricate and interesting

12. The best songs are a) simple and elegant b) complex compositions c) ones that make you feel something

13. When it comes to reading, I prefer a) nonfiction that helps me understand the world better b) anything that captures my attention c) fiction that brings characters to life

14. The best visual art is a) the most exquisitely structured b) not really something I care about c) the most personally expressive

15. When it comes to movies, I enjoy plots that a) unfold slowly and intricately, but make perfect sense in the end b) are based in reality, like documentaries c) can be interpreted in many ways

KEY

1. a) 1 b) 3 c) 2
2. a) 3 b) 1 c) 2
3. a) 1 b) 2 c) 3
4. a) 1 b) 3 c) 2
5. a) 3 b) 2 c) 1

6. a) 3 b) 2 c) 1
7. a) 2 b) 3 c) 1
8. a) 1 b) 3 c) 2
9. a) 2 b) 1 c) 3
10. a) 2 b) 3 c) 1
11. a) 3 b) 1 c) 2

12. a) 2 b) 3 c) 1
13. a) 3 b) 2 c) 1
14. a) 3 b) 2 c) 1
15. a) 3 b) 2 c) 1

Total ____

RESULTS

15–24 points
Like M.C. ESCHER, you are highly RIGHT-BRAINED and very passion-ate! You are comfortable with problems that lack definite answers. For example, you think that different people can have different but valid opinions about things, and that the best way to solve big problems is for people to understand one another. You approach your life in spontaneous, often unexpected ways. You may be a bit of a romantic.

25–34 points
Like MICHELANGELO, you are somewhere BETWEEN RIGHT-BRAINED AND LEFT-BRAINED. For you, beauty can be both orderly and surprising. You understand how two people can see the world differently, but you feel that there's a right or a wrong answer most of the time. You prefer for your surroundings to be under control, but not so much that they become dull.

35–45 points
Like COPERNICUS, you are highly LEFT-BRAINED, with strong opinions and an even stronger will. You love math and logic, and you don't understand people who live by their emotions, because emotions can be misguiding. You prefer to have everything in its place. You always want to have a plan and to see it through to the end. You get pleasure out of learning facts.

Which Music Genre Tunes You in?

1. My favorite line from any song a) is perfectly sweet and poetic
   b) is great because of the way the singer inflects it
   c) expresses something very complex and dark

2. A great singer a) writes ALL of his or her own words b) might
   rely on someone else to write the words—it's the delivery
   that counts c) writes some of the lyrics, but depends on
   bandmates as well

3. A great singer a) uses lots of cool effects in the studio
   b) uses effects, but subtly c) uses no effects—a talented
   singer doesn't need any help

4. My favorite singers a) may or may not play instruments—it's
   up to them b) have to play instruments if they want to be taken
   seriously c) shouldn't do anything other than sing—why
   get distracted?

5. I love when the lyrics are delivered a) loudly and aggressively
   b) sweetly and tenderly c) with real personality

6. My favorite songs are a) an equal blend of all the instrumental
   sections b) heavy on drums and rhythm c) mostly melodic

7. I prefer genres that a) say a lot with words b) can get me
   pumped up c) stoke my imagination

8. My favorite musicians a) should be able to play with technical
   perfection b) don't have to be the best, as long as they can
   reach me emotionally c) should be above average if they want
   me to listen, but don't have to be virtuosos

9. I like hearing music a) anywhere—I don't care about the speakers b) on the best speakers possible c) on speakers with heavy bass

10. When it comes to instrumental solos, a) count me out b) I live for them c) they're OK, as long as they're short and sweet

11. When I go to a concert, I expect that a) the show could start at any hour, without notice b) things will go precisely as listed in the program c) things will start a little late, but not too late

12. When it comes to dancing, a) I'm the first one out on the floor b) I wouldn't even go to a concert where there was dancing c) you might get me out for a cut or two

13. I mostly go to concerts at a) big venues where I can pack a picnic b) small, intimate clubs c) places where there's no curfew

14. In addition to the music, I expect a) commentary from the conductor b) awesome pyrotechnics c) cheap beer

15. I expect my fellow concertgoers to a) react to the performance however they want b) stay silent—at most, clapping politely at the end c) jump around and have fun—concerts are just as much about the crowd as they are about the musicians

16. My favorite musicians a) have big egos and show off b) say everything they need to say with their music c) are interesting people, but not total divas

17. I listen to music that features a) full groups of equally talented musicians b) certain standout musicians, at times c) one superstar who carries everyone else

18. I expect my favorite musicians to a) talk to me after the show, as if we could be friends b) tower over me c) acknowledge their fans, but not mingle with them too much

19. On the cover of my favorite album is a) a larger-than-life picture of the band's leader b) the whole band c) some other picture altogether

20. If my favorite musician is sad, I would expect a) to get a sense of it in the songs b) to be hit over the head with it in every song c) to not know—I don't want them to stop making me happy

KEY

1. a) 3 b) 2 c) 1
2. a) 1 b) 3 c) 2
3. a) 3 b) 2 c) 1
4. a) 2 b) 1 c) 3
5. a) 1 b) 3 c) 2
6. a) 2 b) 3 c) 1
7. a) 2 b) 1 c) 3
8. a) 1 b) 3 c) 2
9. a) 1 b) 3 c) 2
10. a) 3 b) 1 c) 2
11. a) 3 b) 1 c) 2
12. a) 3 b) 1 c) 2
13. a) 1 b) 2 c) 3
14. a) 1 b) 3 c) 2
15. a) 2 b) 1 c) 3
16. a) 1 b) 3 c) 2
17. a) 3 b) 2 c) 1
18. a) 3 b) 1 c) 2
19. a) 1 b) 2 c) 3
20. a) 2 b) 1 c) 3

Total ____

RESULTS

20–27 points
You are best suited to CLASSICAL and OPERA. You appreciate skill and refined taste. Rules are good in composition as well as performance. Leave experimentation for the practice room. You listen to music to hear things you would never be able to do yourself.

28–35 points
You are best suited to ROCK and HEAVY METAL. Your musical taste suggests a complex personality that combines individuality with a need for control. You believe in the power of one person to do big

things in art and life, and you expect talented people to be ambitious without shame.

36–44 points

You are best suited to POP and TOP 40. Music should be the sound track to a party—fun, danceable, and pleasurable for everyone. You don't care too much about how the music is made, as long as it can get you feeling good.

45–52 points

You are best suited to SOUL and HIP-HOP. Musicians are special people, and they deserve their time in the spotlight. But the main thing is the music. After signing a few autographs, it's time to get down to business. You connect with musicians (and other people in general) when you really believe that they're dedicated to what they're doing. You appreciate authenticity, and you are quick to smell a rat when someone is posturing.

53–60 points

You are best suited to ELECTRONIC, JAZZ, and INDIE. Music is a hard thing to pin down, and you won't be the one to try to explain it with words. You listen because you want to feel things you can't feel elsewhere in your life. Who cares about a musician's personal life? If she's not making you dance or cry, she's not doing her job. You're drawn to artists whose personalities come out almost entirely in their music. Experiencing the crowd is the best part of going to a concert— or any event, for that matter.

Which Mode of Transportation Drives You?

1. Other people are a) the most fascinating thing in the world b) usually in my way c) fine in moderation

2. When I work, I a) am highly efficient b) get the job done, I guess c) often end up doing something different from what I set out to do

3. I prefer to combat boredom by a) zoning out b) becoming attuned to the world around me c) thinking about exciting things

4. In general, I prefer to control my life by a) not getting bogged down b) always knowing what I'm doing ahead of time c) guarding my own personal space

5. I am a) romantic b) pragmatic c) somewhere in-between

6. I prefer to spend time with my friends a) out on the town b) on prolonged adventures c) at one of our homes

7. If I have some free time, I'm most likely to a) read or play a game b) catch up on current events c) explore something new

8. The environment is a) something that should be protected b) not exactly my biggest concern right now c) something people should be in better touch with

9. Material possessions are a) mostly a burden b) fun! c) often necessary, but not the most important thing in life

10. The most exciting things to watch are a) driven by plots b) human interactions c) natural images

11. Which of the following images is the most immediately appealing to your eye?

a)  b) c)

KEY

1. a) 1 b) 3 c) 2

2. a) 3 b) 1 c) 2

3. a) 3 b) 1 c) 2

4. a) 2 b) 1 c) 3

5. a) 2 b) 3 c) 1

6. a) 1 b) 2 c) 3

7. a) 1 b) 3 c) 2

8. a) 1 b) 3 c) 2

9. a) 2 b) 3 c) 1

10. a) 3 b) 1 c) 2

11. a) 6 b) 9 c) 3

Total ____

RESULTS

13–17 points

You are best suited to BIKING or WALKING. Why rush to get some-place quickly when you can take in the scenery? Bikes may be slow, but there's nothing like having the wind in your hair as you move. Plus, you get great exercise.

18–23 points

You are best suited to MASS TRANSIT, such as subways and buses. You are something of a city person, preferring the company of many other people to a tightly contained private space. Your habits and interests make you a good fit for transport that gets you where you need to go efficiently, cheaply, and in an environmentally friendly way. Mass transit runs on a regular schedule, so you can easily plan your trips; but at the same time, you don't have to run the vehicles yourself, leaving you time for your own pursuits.

24–29 points
You are best suited to TRAINS and BOATS. For you, transportation is less about getting somewhere and more about the journey itself. You love the romance of traveling long distances and seeing new things, and you might meet some new people along the way. Who knows where your trip will take you? You are not concerned with efficiency, and you like to keep your options open overall.

30–34 points
You are best suited to AIRPLANES. You like the efficiency of air travel, and you have no problem staying distracted during delays. You prefer not to have to operate your travel vehicle, so you can read or seek out other entertainment instead. Keep logging those miles!

35–39 points
You are best suited to CARS. Transportation is all about getting from point A to point B. Whatever you need to do to make that happen smoothly, you're on it. You prefer having the freedom to get your work done unhindered by petty annoyances. You value privacy and personal space. You keep the worlds of work and leisure as separate as you can.

Does Your Name Fit Your Personality?

1. Have you ever changed your first name or switched between the long version and a nickname? a) Yes b) No

2. Your friends call you a) by your name b) by a nickname, initials, or a variation on your first name c) by your last name

3. You sign casual emails a) with your whole first name b) with one letter or initials c) some other way

4. When you meet other people who have your name, a) you get excited b) you feel territorial c) you don't believe them—your name is unique

5. You find that your name is a) easy to say and easy for people to understand b) kind of hard to communicate over the phone c) so difficult for people to understand that you often use other names for restaurant reservations and such

6. Your first name is a) one syllable b) two syllables c) three syllables or more

7. Your first name is a) the same as one of your parents' names b) very similar to a relative or family friend's name c) kind of out of the blue

8. Your first name begins with a) a soft consonant, like the F in Fred or the N in Neil b) a hard consonant, like the K in Kate or the D in Dan c) a vowel sound

9. Your first name ends with a) a soft consonant, like the L in Bill or the M in Tom b) a hard consonant, like the B in Bob or the C in Eric c) a vowel sound

10. Your first name is a) mostly consonants b) mostly vowels c) about half and half

11. Your name a) has great significance in your family b) has religious or cultural significance c) is just a name

12. Your name is a) an everyday English word (like Grace or Faith) b) similar to an everyday English word (like Serena) c) just a name

13. Your name has a) an important meaning in another language b) no meaning that you know of

14. Your name is a) very traditional—you know lots of other people who have it b) modern—you've met a few people who have it, but they're mostly your age or younger c) totally unique

15. Other people a) often ask what your name means, or where it came from b) don't ask about your name very often

KEY

1. a) 2 b) 4
2. a) 2 b) 3 c) 1
3. a) 3 b) 2 c) 1
4. a) 3 b) 1 c) 2
5. a) 3 b) 2 c) 1

Total____

6. a) 1 b) 2 c) 3
7. a) 1 b) 2 c) 3
8. a) 2 b) 1 c) 3
9. a) 2 b) 1 c) 3
10. a) 1 b) 3 c) 2
11. a) 1 b) 2 c) 3
12. a) 1 b) 2 c) 3
13. a) 2 b) 1
14. a) 3 b) 2 c) 1
15. a) 2 b) 1

Total____

RESULTS

The score from your first five answers will determine your name comfort.

6–9 points You are somewhat uncomfortable with your name.

10–12 points You are mostly comfortable with your name.

13–16 points You are very comfortable with, even proud of, your name.

The score from the remaining answers will determine what your name says to others.

10–13 points
Your name is CLASSIC, never out of style. Easy to pronounce, easy to remember, your name is popular with every generation. It suggests that you're easygoing and personable, and probably very honest as well.

14–17 points
Your name is TRADITIONAL, loaded with personal or family meaning. People respect its simplicity. Your name indicates directness, and it confers an air of authority and confidence.

18–20 points
Your name is HIGHLY RECOGNIZABLE, trendy around the time you were born, but just different enough to be intriguing. Your name implies that you balance your life well.

21–24 points
Your name is CUTTING EDGE, though you know some other people who have it. Since so few people have your name, others identify it with you. You stand out in a crowd and command attention.

25–28 points
Your name is UNIQUE. Upon hearing it, people want to know your story. It is a name that suggests ingenuity and freedom and the possibility of breaking out of familiar molds. You have rare personality traits that anyone who has met you can recognize from a mile away. You are a great storyteller.

What Does Your Taste in Clothes Expose About You?

Circle the pattern that you would most like to have on the following items of clothing.

1. Sweater
   a) ☰ horizontal stripes
   b) ||| vertical stripes
   c) ⫻ diagonal stripes

2. Pants
   a) ■ solid color
   b) ||| pin stripes
   c) ||| heavy stripes

3. Socks
   a) ◆ argyle
   b) ■ solid color
   c) ⣿ polka dots

4. Jacket
   a) 🍀 camouflage
   b) ||| stripes
   c) 🐆 leopard print

5. T-shirt
   a) ■ solid color
   b) ☀ nature image
   c) ▢ geometric design

6. I own the most a) business clothes b) going-out clothes c) around-the-house clothes

7. I own an outfit I could wear to an important interview.
   a) Yes b) No

8. My closet is filled with a) things I probably don't really need b) a comfortable amount of stuff c) tons of great options that can be mixed and matched for any occasion

9. Style-wise, I still like to wear things I owned five or even ten years ago. a) Yes b) No

10. Circle all that qualify. I own an obsessive amount of a) shoes b) hats c) shirts

11. When it comes to new fashions, I a) pay close attention b) pay no attention whatsoever c) keep my eyes open, but don't go too far with it

12. I shop to manage my mood a) sometimes b) rarely, if ever c) as often as I can afford it

13. When I'm at the mall, I a) am totally in my element b) get what I need, and that's about it c) feel a little anxious

14. I replace old clothes a) when they get worn out b) when they go totally out of fashion c) the minute I see something even slightly better

15. I usually shop for clothes a) with friends b) by myself c) either with friends or by myself

KEY

1. a) 2 b) 1 c) 3

2. a) 1 b) 2 c) 3

3. a) 2 b) 1 c) 3

4. a) 2 b) 1 c) 3

5. a) 1 b) 3 c) 2

6. a) 2 b) 3 c) 1

7. a) 3 b) 1

8. a) 2 b) 1 c) 3

9. a) 1 b) 3

10. 2 points for each

11. a) 3 b) 1 c) 2

12. a) 2 b) 1 c) 3

13. a) 3 b) 2 c) 1

14. a) 1 b) 2 c) 3

15. a) 3 b) 1 c) 2

Total ____

RESULTS

14–20 points
Your style is CASUAL. You are mostly unconcerned with clothing. You put yourself first, and that means not worrying too much about others' perceptions. You're not a plain person, but you don't need to advertise yourself as "interesting."

21–27 points
You dress CONSERVATIVELY. If possible, you would wear a uniform—in other words, if you could wear the same outfit every day, that would be ideal. You are an extremely private person.

28–34 points
Your style is PREPPY or CLASSIC. You are somewhat concerned with clothing. You don't define yourself by material possessions, but you feel that it's important as a member of society to keep up with what's happening in the world—and sometimes that means buying new things.

35–41 points
Your style is HIGH FASHION. You really love clothing and will go out on a limb with designs and spending. You are generally outgoing, and you pay close attention to personalities and relationships. You are a seize-the-moment type who wants to impress people and go places in life.

42–48 points
Your style is BOHEMIAN. Fashion is a chance for you to express yourself. You prefer to get funky items from the thrift store or make your own clothes—because they let you be different. You enjoy entertaining people and going places no one has gone before.

What Kind of Professional Athlete Would You Be?

Choose the image that appeals to you most.

1. a) ◯   b) ☐   c) ▭
2. a) ◇   b) ☐   c) ◯
3. a) ⚫   b) ◯   c) ⬬

4. When it comes to rules, a) the more there are, the more interesting the game b) there should be just enough to keep the game orderly c) they're made to be broken

5. You are most comfortable a) thinking a move or two ahead in any game b) thinking many moves ahead c) totally winging it

6. Authority figures a) exist to enforce rules and should be around as often as possible b) should be called upon strictly when necessary c) should be avoided at all costs

7. You tend to enjoy things that a) make sense right off the bat b) take years and years to really understand c) are complex enough to be interesting, but not so difficult to figure out in a short amount of time

8. People work together most effectively when they a) have a little help from a leader b) are organized by a single, powerful leader c) have total personal autonomy

9. You are best at accomplishing tasks a) with a helping hand when necessary b) all by yourself c) with a group of people

10. Teammates a) are there for you always b) are there for you today, but could theoretically change allegiances at some point c) can never completely be trusted

11. If a teammate is missing, a) you do your best to compensate by taking on new responsibilities b) it doesn't matter, you can swap someone else in c) the chemistry of the team may be thrown off altogether

12. A teammate is someone who a) can fill in for you when you're tired b) does a specialized job completely different from yours c) may be competing with you for glory

13. You prefer to communicate with people you work with by a) knowing exactly what you're doing ahead of time b) talking a lot while you work

KEY

1. a) 3 b) 2 c) 1	**5.** a) 2 b) 3 c) 1	**10.** a) 1 b) 2 c) 3
2. a) 2 b) 1 c) 3	**6.** a) 1 b) 2 c) 3	**11.** a) 1 b) 2 c) 3
3. a) 1 b) 2 c) 3	**7.** a) 1 b) 3 c) 2	**12.** a) 3 b) 2 c) 1
4. a) 3 b) 2 c) 1	**8.** a) 1 b) 2 c) 3	**13.** a) 2 b) 1
	9. a) 2 b) 3 c) 1	Total ____

RESULTS

13–17 points
You would function best as a BASKETBALL, SOCCER, or HOCKEY player. You are team oriented, and you appreciate the value of collaborating with other people to maximize the value of everyone's skills. You like games that are relatively simple in design but complex in execution. You prefer for rules to be strictly enforced, as they often are by referees in all three sports.

18–22 points

You would function best as a BASEBALL, VOLLEYBALL, or FOOTBALL player. You enjoy having teammates, but you are most comfortable when everyone has a very specialized job to do. You work best under strong leaders, such as managers and coaches, who can handle most of the strategizing in advance, leaving you to carry out instructions.

23–27 points

You would excel most in SWIMMING, TRACK-AND-FIELD, TENNIS, or CYCLING. You don't mind alternating with a partner, but you don't necessarily want to collaborate with them directly. Once the competition begins, you want to be on your own.

28–33 points

You would function best as a RACECAR DRIVER or GOLFER. You like to work in total silence, or at least in your own private space. You enjoy competing on specialized courses that change from place to place. You are not so excited about playing with teammates—you're more focused on attaining a personal best score or time.

34–38 points

You would be strongest as a MARATHON RUNNER, PROFESSIONAL WRESTLER, or TRIATHLETE. You are an independent spirit, and you prefer to trust the outcome of a game to your own skills, rather than a team's. You may even be somewhat suspicious of the idea of teammates. You may see authority figures, such as referees, as a hindrance, and you may try to operate without them seeing what you're doing. Furthermore, you don't need a leader to tell you the game plan—you'll figure it out yourself.

1. When it comes to family, you prefer to a) see them sometimes, but not too often b) live in the same house or neighborhood c) live as far away as possible

2. You have (or want to have) a) several children b) just enough children you can comfortably support c) one child or no children

3. Your family includes a) just a few immediate relatives b) several immediate relatives c) lots of relatives, as well as friends whom you consider family

4. For birthdays and holidays, you a) send wishes by email b) are often too busy to remember c) try to throw parties, or at least attend them

5. The obligations of family include a) staying out of each other's way b) playing an active, supportive role in each other's lives c) contributing to the family financially

6. Breakfast is a) important fuel for the day b) usually something like a vitamin pill and a breakfast bar c) a great time to gather with people

7. Food should be prepared a) slowly and lovingly b) with the most convenient gadgets available c) by people working in restaurants

8. Thanksgiving dinner is great for a) inviting people you want to network with b) getting the whole clan together c) trying out fancy new kitchen tools

9. Lunch is a) a nice, long break, preferably followed by a nap b) something I do at my desk c) usually heated very quickly in a microwave

10. Restaurants are a) way more efficient than cooking on your own b) fine, as long as you can get takeout c) great, as long as you can take up a table for a couple of hours and talk

11. I work a) because I just can't imagine not working b) as little as possible—it isn't a big part of my life c) to contribute toward progress on a greater scale

12. Big business a) makes me a little uncomfortable b) is the backbone of the economy c) leads to important new discoveries in many fields

13. Businesses should a) really try hard to be good to their workers b) pay people, and that's enough c) make sure their employees feel like part of the team

14. Money a) is the root of all evil b) is the most important thing in the world (or close to it) c) should be invested in new technologies

15. At work, an employee should dress a) to the nines—you want to impress people b) like everyone else c) in whatever way feels most comfortable

KEY

1. a) 2 b) 1 c) 3
2. a) 1 b) 2 c) 3
3. a) 3 b) 2 c) 1
4. a) 3 b) 2 c) 1
5. a) 3 b) 1 c) 2
6. a) 2 b) 3 c) 1
7. a) 1 b) 3 c) 2
8. a) 2 b) 1 c) 3
9. a) 1 b) 2 c) 3
10. a) 3 b) 2 c) 1
11. a) 2 b) 1 c) 3
12. a) 1 b) 2 c) 3
13. a) 1 b) 2 c) 3
14. a) 1 b) 2 c) 3
15. a) 3 b) 2 c) 1

Total _____

RESULTS

15–25 points
You would live most naturally in a TRADITIONAL CULTURE. You value relationships more highly than personal success or general economic progress. You like to take your time and to contemplate the world around you. You appreciate leisure and love, and you are suspicious of things that take time away from them. You would prefer to work directly in the service of your friends and family than for a big, faceless company. You like longstanding rituals and are happy to participate in celebratory events. If you could, you would like to live more simply.

26–34 points
You would operate most smoothly in a WORKAHOLIC CULTURE. Your family matters, but that doesn't mean you want to spend all day with them. Your job takes over many aspects of your life, and that's not necessarily a bad thing—you believe in what you do, and it keeps you locked into a regular routine. Sometimes, you even feel like family business gets in the way of things you should be working on. You might be happiest in a society where your main contribution is as part of the workforce. Meals and rituals are things you would rather scale down to the bare minimum.

35–45 points
You would excel in a super-modern, HIGH-TECH CULTURE. You enjoy people, food, and art, but all of those things are most exciting when there's a new toy to play with. You look forward to seeing what human ingenuity and science are capable of creating, and you spend a lot of time thinking about new technologies. When you work, you want to be contributing to thrilling new types of progress—conveniences and leisure devices that will improve all of our lives. You would be happiest in a society that shares your excitement. What Supernatural Creature Would You Be?

Which Supernatural Creature Would You Be?

1. When you were in high school, you were a a) normal kid
   b) jock c) nerd

2. The most important trait in making friends is a) charm
   b) flexibility c) being outgoing

3. On a lazy Sunday with friends, you prefer to a) sit inside and
   drink coffee b) play a sport c) make plans for the whole day

4. Dressing to the nines a) is irrelevant b) can get people
   to notice you c) is the best way to move up in the world

5. You a) have a few friends who were once close, but aren't
   anymore b) remain close with all your friends c) have fallen
   out with a lot of friends

6. Whatever doesn't kill you a) only makes you stronger
   b) can still hurt a bit c) can still really sting!

7. When you have a mosquito bite, you a) scratch it constantly
   b) scratch it a little c) barely pay attention

8. You're allergic to a) nothing b) several things c) a few things

9. When people say hurtful things, you are a) affected for a brief
   time b) unaffected, usually c) affected for a long time

10. Strong flavors are a) delicious b) too much for you c) fine,
    in limited amounts

11. When you hang around different groups of people, you find that
    your way of speaking changes a) often b) rarely c) sometimes

12. You get really, rip-roarin' angry a) often b) sometimes c) rarely

13. Your emotional side a) comes out sometimes b) is nonexistent
    c) is always on display

14. When it comes to strange situations you a) feel uncomfortable b) keep your head down c) figure out ways to fit in

15. When you want to do one thing and a friend wants to do another, you a) often put your foot down b) graciously defer to them c) try to compromise

KEY

1. a) 2 b) 1 c) 3
2. a) 3 b) 2 c) 1
3. a) 2 b) 1 c) 3
4. a) 1 b) 2 c) 3
5. a) 2 b) 1 c) 3
6. a) 1 b) 2 c) 3
7. a) 3 b) 2 c) 1
8. a) 1 b) 3 c) 2
9. a) 2 b) 1 c) 3
10. a) 1 b) 3 c) 2
11. a) 3 b) 1 c) 2
12. a) 1 b) 2 c) 3
13. a) 2 b) 3 c) 1
14. a) 2 b) 1 c) 3
15. a) 1 b) 3 c) 2
Total _____

RESULTS

15–25
You would walk the earth forever as a ZOMBIE. You are direct and often stubborn. You see your way as the best way and don't want to budge. Your methods are simple and honest.

26–34
You would terrorize the living as a WEREWOLF. You're an honest person, but there are some things you just don't want people to know. Certain things—foods, pet peeves—can quickly change your mood.

35–45
You would spend an unholy eternity as a VAMPIRE. You look out for number one and use wit and charm, rather than force, to get what you want. You are very sensitive to some objects and things people say.

Chapter **2**: YOU + OTHERS

Are You Judgmental?

1. Fashion is **a)** a great way to express yourself **b)** not really my world **c)** totally obnoxious

2. When you wear an item of clothing from a brand-name designer, you should **a)** wear it proudly **b)** hide the logo entirely **c)** be a little subtle about it

3. Young people today are **a)** the same as young people of any generation **b)** cause for concern **c)** a fascinating bunch

4. Eyeglasses **a)** can be a cool fashion statement **b)** are a sign of intelligence **c)** usually don't look that great, in my opinion

5. Very tall children **a)** might have trouble fitting in, at times **b)** are obviously eating a great diet **c)** will be well respected by their peers

6. When you want to get together but a friend is busy, you **a)** often try to convince them to come out anyway **b)** immediately let it go **c)** might prod them a little bit, but not too much

7. When a friend's house is unusually dirty, you **a)** might ask if everything is OK **b)** wonder why **c)** get very concerned

8. You think of yourself as highly capable of judging character. **a)** Yes **b)** No

9. People who have different musical taste from you **a)** have something really interesting to offer you in conversation **b)** are often hard for you to relate to **c)** are just different in one way—it's not a big deal

10. People who wear really nice clothes **a)** probably have a lot of money **b)** must be putting on airs **c)** must like dressing well

11. At the grocery store, you see a new type of butter with a really bright label, and it costs a dollar less than your usual brand. You a) give it a try—after all, it's cheap b) assume the bright label means they're making up for bad quality c) give it a try—after all, it's new

12. When selecting a sports teammate from a group of people you don't know, you would a) try to watch during warm-ups to see who is the best player b) look at physical size and shape c) try to figure out who looks like "the sporting type"

13. When engaged in small talk, you a) try to move the conversation somewhere more interesting as soon as possible b) try to get out of the conversation quickly c) often get overwhelmed by how boring it is

14. Someone asks you for change on the street. You a) suspect that the person is faking poverty b) try to determine how much they actually need it before giving anything c) give something if you feel like it, even if that's rarely

15. The new mayoral candidate of your city comes from another city. You wonder a) how he got to know your city so quickly b) whether he knows enough about the city to be a politician here c) who he is and what he stands for

KEY

1. a) 3 b) 1 c) 2
2. a) 3 b) 2 c) 1
3. a) 2 b) 3 c) 1
4. a) 2 b) 3 c) 1
5. a) 1 b) 3 c) 2

6. a) 3 b) 1 c) 2
7. a) 1 b) 2 c) 3
8. a) 3 b) 1
9. a) 1 b) 3 c) 2
10. a) 2 b) 3 c) 1
11. a) 1 b) 3 c) 2

12. a) 1 b) 2 c) 3
13. a) 1 b) 2 c) 3
14. a) 3 b) 2 c) 1
15. a) 2 b) 3 c) 1

Total ____

RESULTS

15–20 points

You are FREETHINKING. You don't take superficial information at face value, preferring to learn more before deciding what you think. You have a live-and-let-live attitude about the world. On the negative side, you might sometimes miss things that more critical people will pick up on. Be careful not to let real problems go unnoticed just because you don't want to interfere.

21–26 points

You are OPEN-MINDED. You work hard not to be judgmental and that means getting the whole story every time. People respect you for your skills as a mediator. You would make a great diplomat or politician!

27–33 points

You are FAIR in your judgments of others. You are good at distinguishing between real information and self-imposed judgments. You don't form concrete opinions about others right away, but you definitely keep your eyes open.

34–39 points

You are CRITICAL. You are not only willing to make judgments, but you're also willing to express them. Honesty is the best policy. You see yourself as a strong judge of character, and you are often inclined to give people the advice they need to hear, even when it might be a little awkward.

40–45 points

You are JUDGMENTAL. You are prone to taking things at face value. You have fairly fixed sets of assumptions that you associate with a fixed set of signs. This might make you appear insular; on the other hand, you most likely have a well-developed eye for the subtle ways people express themselves with their bodies and clothing.

Do You Care What Others Think of You?

1. When you look in the mirror in the morning, you look for
   a) all the things you need to fix b) food between your teeth
   c) a fleeting moment, just because it's there

2. When you look in the mirror in the morning, you stand there
   for a) less than two minutes b) less than ten minutes c) ten
   minutes or more

3. You regularly use a) one mirror b) two mirrors c) more than
   two mirrors

4. When getting ready for a night on the town, you a) check
   yourself out from every possible angle b) just glance quickly
   c) check yourself out from one or two angles

5. A mirror is a) a normal, useful device b) bad for your
   self-image c) a total necessity

6. You fish for compliments a) rarely, if ever b) once in a while
   c) often

7. When flattered, you respond by a) politely thanking the person
   who flattered you b) becoming shy c) insisting it isn't true

8. When people insult you, they usually do so a) directly
   b) subtly—you have to pay attention c) rarely, if ever

9. If someone says something unkind to you, you a) tell them you
   feel hurt b) plan to get back at them c) lose respect for them

10. If you're probably never going to see someone again, you
    a) treat them as you would anyone else in your life b) keep
    your interaction with them as brief as possible c) try to be
    extra nice, just because

11. Circle all of the following that apply. You rely heavily on your friends a) for validation about the way your body looks b) for validation about the way you dress c) for perspective on your romantic relationships d) to tell you about parties and other social events e) to tell you when you're being unreasonable

KEY

1. a) 3 b) 1 c) 2

2. a) 1 b) 2 c) 3

3. a) 1 b) 2 c) 3

4. a) 3 b) 1 c) 2

5. a) 1 b) 2 c) 3

6. a) 1 b) 2 c) 3

7. a) 1 b) 2 c) 3

8. a) 1 b) 3 c) 2

9. a) 1 b) 3 c) 2

10. a) 2 b) 1 c) 3

11. Add the following points for each item circled. a) 3 b) 3 c) 1 d) 0 e) 2

Total ____

RESULTS

10–15 points

You are CLUELESS about how others see you—maybe on purpose! This can be good or bad. On one hand, you are confident enough to live your life in the way that makes you happiest. You put your needs first. You don't stress about other people's perceptions of you, and you're not overly self-concious. On the other hand, you may miss some useful feedback from people you care about—these cues can sometimes be important for maintaining happy relationships.

16–21 points

You are INDIFFERENT to the way that others see you. You are well adjusted and confident, but every once in a while, you'll become self-aware, especially around people you really care about. Still, you're usually able to go about your daily business without getting too bogged down in trying to look or act cool.

22–27 points

You are SELF-AWARE about how others see you. You are attuned to social standards and to the way you will be perceived. You adjust your interactions and behaviors to make yourself look good, but you don't take things so far that it makes you anxious or takes up a ton of your time. When it comes to important events such as attending a wedding, you might spend some serious time thinking about your appearance; but on a day-to-day basis, you're fairly laid-back. You are your own person, but you're aware that your loved ones sometimes need you to be flexible about the way you act.

28–33 points

You are CONCERNED with the way others see you. While it doesn't completely ruin your life, you really can't help imagining an audience for everything you do, from buying clothes to reading books to hanging out with friends. You are deeply bothered by gossip and often worried that you might be the focus of it. Sometimes you find yourself getting a little paranoid. On the plus side, people think of you as thoughtful and considerate, and you are a good friend.

34–39 points

You are PREOCCUPIED with how others see you. You tailor your personality, as well as your wardrobe, to satisfy others and give them the best impression possible. This suggests a high level of self-awareness, which is both good and bad. On one hand, you are very attuned to what your loved ones need from you, and you can be a very giving friend. On the other, you cause yourself some distress by not asserting your own needs strongly enough. Be sure to follow your instincts and to let your personality shine through.

How Well Do You Read Faces and Body Language?

Look at the following pictures. Spending thirty seconds on each picture, write down what cues (boredom, interest, disbelief, etc.) you would "read" if the person were real and having a conversation with you. Write down as much as you can.

1. _____

2. _____

3. _____

4. _____

5. _____

KEY

To find your total, tally the number of cues you picked up on based on the descriptions below. It's all right if you used different words, as long as you noted something very similar.

1. A tug on the ear may mean that the listener does not believe what you're saying (**2 points**). It also indicates that he has stopped paying attention (**1 point**).

2. Scratching the back of the head often indicates that the person is feeling impatient with you (**2 points**). It may also indicate that he is not paying attention to you (**1 point**).

3. Touching of the chin indicates that the person is interested in what you said and is thinking about it (**2 points**). In rarer cases, it may mean the person is bored or sleepy, and he is propping the chin up with his hand to keep his head from drooping (**1 point**).

4. Raised eyebrows indicate that the person is skeptical about what you're saying or that he outright disagrees with you (**2 points**). In rarer instances, the person just might be confused (**1 point**).

5. Crossed arms most often indicate hostility, opposition, or standoff-ishness (**2 points**). In extremely rare cases, it simply indicates that the person is cold (**1 point**).

RESULTS

0–5 points
You are ILLITERATE when it comes to reading body language and facial expressions. It may be that you focus more on words than on non-linguistic expression. If you find yourself in a lot of awkward verbal exchanges with people, you may want to pay more attention to what their faces, arms, and bodily poses are implying.

6–11 points
You are AWARE of body language and facial expressions. You understand most of the overt signals, but perhaps miss some of the more subtle ones. You are good at getting more emotional information from people than they openly express; however, you're not so good at often anticipating how your remarks will be received in advance.

12–15 points
You are OBSERVANT of body language and facial expressions. You are a true expert at spotting small hints that speakers themselves may have no idea they're dropping. In business conversations, you learn a lot of valuable information, and you have a keen eye in romantic encounters as well.

What's Your Emotional IQ?

1. Your best friend tells you she got a raise at work. You a) give her a huge hug or handshake b) ask her how much c) comment about whether you think you'll get a raise soon, too

2. A relative calls to tell you he just got engaged. You a) immediately ask when the wedding will be b) give useful advice about wedding preparations c) tell him how glad you are for him

3. A friend informs you that she just got into a great college or graduate program. You just got rejected from one. You a) tell her you're happy for her, and then let her know what happened to you b) tell her you're happy for her, without mentioning what happened to you c) immediately open up about what happened to you

4. You are happiest when you a) achieve something big in your life b) spend time with people you love c) can make others happy

5. People most often express their happiness by a) talking about it directly b) being positive toward others in their lives c) making wise and constructive choices

6. A friend who has never given you very good advice asks *you* for advice. You a) politely say you don't think you're able to help b) give some advice, but hold back a bit c) give advice as well as you can

7. Your romantic partner wants to go on a vacation to a place where you're not interested in going. You a) hide the fact that you don't want to go, and try to seem like you're having fun in order to make your partner happy b) state clearly and directly that this trip is not for you c) explain that you are skeptical, but will try it out for your partner's sake

8. A friend asks if you know anyone he might be able to go on a date with. You first consider a) other friends who might be available b) what kind of traits your friend might be looking for in a partner c) why your friend asked you instead of someone else

9. Your best friend talks much more than you. You a) don't mind—people have different personalities b) sometimes wish your friend would give you more room to talk c) try to even things out whenever you notice the disparity

10. You have a) many friends, but few close ones b) an average number of friends, and some close ones c) almost exclusively close friends, and few casual ones

11. You have an argument with a friend. After the fight, you a) think about how you might have made your point more clearly b) try to think about something else for a little while c) think about what the other person said

12. Two of your relatives are having a silly feud. You a) explain to them that they're being silly b) try to stay out of it c) ask to hear both sides

13. A good friend confides in you about a problem that you yourself have never experienced. You a) think about why you've never had that problem, and tell your friend what you've done to avoid it b) try to put yourself in your friend's shoes c) politely tell your friend that it wouldn't be fair for you to give advice about a situation you've never been in

14. Conflict is best resolved by a) talking things out b) time c) life-changing situations that let people see what's really important in life

15. Conflict usually arises from a) misunderstanding b) stubbornness c) situations that are out of any one person's control

KEY

1. a) 3 b) 2 c) 1	**6.** a) 2 b) 1 c) 3	**12.** a) 2 b) 1 c) 3
2. a) 2 b) 1 c) 3	**7.** a) 1 b) 2 c) 3	**13.** a) 1 b) 3 c) 2
3. a) 3 b) 2 c) 1	**8.** a) 2 b) 3 c) 1	**14.** a) 3 b) 2 c) 1
4. a) 1 b) 3 c) 2	**9.** a) 2 b) 3 c) 1	**15.** a) 2 b) 1 c) 3
5. a) 1 b) 2 c) 3	**10.** a) 1 b) 3 c) 2	
	11. a) 1 b) 2 c) 3	Total ____

RESULTS

15–22 points
You have a LOW emotional IQ. When giving advice, you often think about yourself instead of trying to empathize with others. Try to think about what others say and, more importantly, why they say it.

23–30 points
You have an AVERAGE emotional IQ. You can manage when it comes to handling emotional friends, but you sometimes fail to be as giving as you can. For example, you could be a good listener, but not the best at deciding how to negotiate a conflict.

31–38 points
You have an ABOVE AVERAGE emotional IQ. You have a strong ability to listen and respond sympathetically when others have problems. You are probably one of the first people your friends come to when they need to talk, either about good or bad news.

39–45 points
You have a GENIUS emotional IQ. You are extremely adept at seeing the world as others do, and you can trace the likely origin of other people's stress quickly and accurately. You can manage your feelings expertly, while often putting your friends or relatives first.

What's Your Love Profile?

1. As a relationship goes on, you tend to a) fight more b) fight less c) fight the same amount

2. As a relationship goes on, you tend to a) go out less b) go out about the same amount c) go out more

3. You have had more than one relationship that lasted a) five years or more b) two years or more c) two weeks or more

4. You have lived with a) more than three romantic partners b) one or two romantic partners c) none of your romantic partners

5. You have moved to a new city to be with someone a) once b) more than once c) never

6. You go out on the town in order to meet potential new partners a) rarely, if ever b) often c) sometimes

7. When single, you find the idea of meeting people a) thrilling b) daunting or exhausting c) somewhat appealing

8. When single, you find yourself looking for someone who a) you might be able to stay with for a while b) can show you a fun time now c) seems interesting

9. When it comes to flirting, you a) do the best you can b) feel pretty nervous c) are a bona fide expert

10. Flirting well requires a) practice b) some innate skill c) confidence

11. Watching a movie at home with a bottle of wine and a date is a) a waste of a night b) often way more fun than it sounds c) a good idea when you don't have the energy to head out

12. Noisy places are a) usually fun b) rarely fun c) sometimes fun, depending on the place and the crowd

13. The best dates are a) well planned b) ones where what you do matters less than who you're with c) totally spontaneous

14. If you're on a date with someone who is down in the dumps, you should a) cheer up your date b) find a new person to go on dates with c) talk to your date and lend a sympathetic ear

15. Cooking for a date is a) too time-consuming b) sensual c) a cute idea

16. After a date, you a) tell everyone you know what happened b) never kiss-and-tell c) blab to your best friend only

17. One of the most important qualities in a potential partner is a) mystery b) intelligence c) to have things in common

18. You fall in love when a) you're good and ready b) you first meet someone c) someone else seems to be falling in love with you first

19. You see yourself a) being with one person forever b) wandering, romantically, forever c) settling down only if you meet the right partner

20. When it comes to anticipating where a relationship will go, you have a) accurate foresight b) terrible foresight c) decent foresight

KEY

1. a) 3 b) 1 c) 2	**7.** a) 3 b) 1 c) 2	**14.** a) 2 b) 3 c) 1
2. a) 1 b) 2 c) 3	**8.** a) 1 b) 3 c) 2	**15.** a) 3 b) 2 c) 1
3. a) 1 b) 2 c) 3	**9.** a) 2 b) 1 c) 3	**16.** a) 3 b) 1 c) 2
4. a) 2 b) 1 c) 3	**10.** a) 3 b) 1 c) 2	**17.** a) 3 b) 2 c) 1
5. a) 2 b) 3 c) 1	**11.** a) 3 b) 1 c) 2	**18.** a) 2 b) 3 c) 1
6. a) 1 b) 3 c) 2	**12.** a) 3 b) 1 c) 2	**19.** a) 1 b) 3 c) 2
	13. a) 2 b) 1 c) 3	**20.** a) 1 b) 3 c) 2

Total ____

RESULTS

20–30 points
You are DEDICATED AND DOMESTIC. You form strong attachments and are likely to be loyal to the person you're with. You don't form many partnerships, but you work hard to make them last. And when you're single, you're likely to rely on your friends to introduce you to new people.

31–40 points
You are CAUTIOUS BUT OPEN. You are interested in committed, long-term relationships, but only if the scenario is right. You want new partners to earn your trust a bit before you open yourself to them, but you're not ultra-demanding. You don't love going out to meet new people, though you understand that it can be a useful strategy. Your relationships develop pronounced patterns but don't become dull.

41–50 points
You are PASSIONATE. You believe in love and pursue it often. But if things aren't going well quickly, you're apt to move on. You don't mind lending an emotional helping hand to a partner, but prefer seeking adventure to playing therapist. You like going out to meet new people, and consider anyone you meet a potential mate. You've made a few bad decisions about romance in the past, but the benefits have been worth it.

51–60 points
You have a DEVIL-MAY-CARE attitude about relationships. You are decidedly uninterested in a long-term partner right now. You go out to meet new people all the time and want to partake in new experiences as often as possible. Routine is not a part of your vocabulary. You enjoy talking about your love life and are fully willing to open yourself to emotional risk for the sake of fun.

How Fulfilling Is Your Current Relationship?

1. When it comes to chores, your partner is most likely to
   a) share b) act independently c) follow your lead

2. You and your partner go out with mutual friends a) often
   b) rarely, if ever c) sometimes

3. When taking trips, you a) always go with your partner b) never
   bring your partner c) sometimes bring your partner

4. Your partner brings you presents a) to make up for things he's
   done wrong b) on all the appropriate birthdays and holidays
   c) at random times

5. I feel surprised by my partner a) every day b) sometimes
   c) rarely, if ever

6. Your partner is a) extremely smart about certain subjects
   b) extremely smart about all subjects c) not that brilliant

7. Your partner teaches you new skills a) every day b) rarely if
   ever c) sometimes

8. When you criticize your partner, it usually results in a) a fight
   b) the same old conversation about the same old problems
   c) your partner learning something from you

9. You and your partner have been to a) many of the same places
   and know many of the same people b) very few of the same
   places and know very few of the same people c) some of the
   same places and know some of the same people

10. You prefer a) listening to your partner b) talking to your partner
    c) when you talk to each other equally

11. You and your partner have a) the same or very similar jobs
    b) wildly different jobs c) different jobs, but not too different

12. You hope to be with your partner for a) the rest of your life b) as long as you're happy together c) a little longer, at least

13. You often feel like you a) know exactly what your partner is going to do b) have no idea what your partner will do next c) have some idea of what your partner is thinking, but are often taken by surprise

14. Your partner is or would be a) a caring parent b) a strong disciplinarian c) amusing to watch as a parent

15. The spaces where you spend time with your partner a) have been designed by the two of you pretty equally b) have been designed mostly by one of you c) somehow just seem to reflect your personality as a couple

KEY

1. a) 3 b) 1 c) 2	**6.** a) 3 b) 1 c) 2	**12.** a) 2 b) 3 c) 1
2. a) 3 b) 1 c) 2	**7.** a) 2 b) 1 c) 3	**13.** a) 1 b) 2 c) 3
3. a) 2 b) 1 c) 3	**8.** a) 2 b) 3 c) 1	**14.** a) 2 b) 1 c) 3
4. a) 1 b) 2 c) 3	**9.** a) 1 b) 3 c) 2	**15.** a) 2 b) 1 c) 3
5. a) 2 b) 3 c) 1	**10.** a) 3 b) 1 c) 2	
	11. a) 2 b) 1 c) 3	Total ____

RESULTS

15–20 points
Your relationship is UNFULFILLING. You take a dim view of your partner and your prospects for the future. You have serious concerns about your prospects of being together for a long time. You either know your partner way too well for things to be interesting, or your partner is hiding some key personality characteristics from you. In any case, your relationship is bringing out the bad side of you.

21–26 points

Your relationship is ADEQUATE. You get along well enough with your partner that your relationship is mostly satisfying. You might fight a little more than you'd like—and maybe he or she isn't exactly who you had pictured you'd be with—but all in all, things are all right. Still, your relationship has quite a few land mines; you have work to do if things are going to improve.

27–33 points

Your relationship is FULFILLING. You enjoy and have a great amount of respect for your partner. You two are thoroughly compatible and deal with each other in a mature and mutually beneficial fashion. Though your relationship isn't perfect, in the end you are a good fit. You learn from each other and are capable of growing together. Hard work will be crucial if you want to continue ironing out the wrinkles, but you have every reason to be optimistic.

34–39 points

Your relationship is GREAT. You couldn't ask for a whole lot more from the person you're with. You really like being around your partner, and you are a better person when you're together. You have a few issues here and there—but then again, doesn't every couple? This relationship has the potential to last a long time, and be very fulfilling.

40–45 points

Your relationship is OUT OF THIS WORLD. You and your partner are a fantastic match. You are emotionally healthy for each other, and you learn a lot from each other, but neither of you dominates the other's personality. Whatever you do together works because you love and respect each other so much. You feel comfortable being together, and your rosy outlook often makes things run even more smoothly, obscuring what otherwise might be difficult patches. Perhaps most importantly, you have a lot of fun.

What Kind of Friend Are You?

1. When asking for advice about something tough, your friends respond best to a) long, detailed opinions b) comments that make them laugh c) your assurances that things will be OK

2. People tend to ask you for advice about a) love b) relationships with friends or family c) general malaise

3. When friends ask you for advice, they usually do it a) over the phone b) in a private setting, such as at dinner or in your house c) over a quick lunch or during a couple of stolen minutes

4. When asked for advice, you try to give it based on a) your own experiences b) what you know of the person asking c) what you consider to be universally good advice

5. You a) love being asked for advice b) like being asked for advice, and mostly take it seriously c) are a little uncomfortable when asked for advice, but try your best

6. You know a) lots and lots of your friends' deepest secrets b) relatively few juicy secrets c) some deep secrets

7. When sworn to secrecy, you blab a) to no one, ever b) rarely, but it does happen c) kind of often, to be honest

8. You enjoy hearing secrets mostly because a) they're so exciting b) you appreciate your friends' trust c) you don't really enjoy hearing secrets

9. You usually share your own secrets with a) no one b) lots of people c) one or two people

10. The longest you've kept a secret is a) a few months, at most b) years and years c) a year or two

11. Your friends more often a) ask you to come along to things b) ask if you have any ideas for things to do

12. You play pranks a) sometimes b) rarely, if ever c) often

13. You tease your friends good-naturedly a) often b) sometimes c) rarely, if ever

14. Your laugh is a) reserved and quiet b) pretty normal c) deep and hearty

15. You are implicated in a) a few of your friends' crazy stories b) a lot of your friends' crazy stories c) no crazy stories—your friends don't really have any

KEY

1. a) 1 b) 2 c) 3

2. a) 1 b) 2 c) 3

3. a) 2 b) 1 c) 3

4. a) 3 b) 1 c) 2

5. a) 2 b) 1 c) 3

6. a) 2 b) 3 c) 1

7. a) 2 b) 1 c) 3

8. a) 3 b) 2 c) 1

9. a) 1 b) 3 c) 2

10. a) 3 b) 2 c) 1

11. a) 1 b) 3

12. a) 2 b) 1 c) 3

13. a) 3 b) 2 c) 1

14. a) 1 b) 2 c) 3

15. a) 2 b) 3 c) 1

Total ____

RESULTS

15–25 points

You are THE SAGE. You are considered wise and thoughtful, and your friends want to know what you have to say about their lives. Whether it's because you're smart or because you pay so much attention to them (or maybe some combination of both!), you are respected for your words of wisdom. When people approach you for advice, they make sure that the setting is appropriate. Although you may be less adept than some people at cracking a joke to break the ice or lighten a heavy situation, you more than make up for it with your keen observations.

26–35 points

You are THE CONFIDANTE. You are considered trustworthy and loyal, and your friends depend on you to give them a sense of stability when times are difficult. You may also be wise and entertaining, but your commitment to friendships is the source of your deepest bonds and your friends' strongest connections to you. People feel that you've never failed them, and they know they can count on you in the future.

36–45 points

You are THE ENTERTAINER. You have a great sense of humor and are often the one who sparks fun ideas and activities. You know that your friends get serious sometimes, and every once in a while they'll bring you in to tell you something or ask you for advice—but a lot of times, you stay out of that stuff. It might make you a little uncomfortable, or you just might not be best at it. In any case, you make your friends feel very good, and they appreciate you for it.

Do People Gossip About You?

1. How many romantic partners have you had in the last five years? a) Less than three b) Three to five c) More than five

2. You travel a) sometimes b) often c) rarely, if ever

3. In the past year, you have been drunk a) less than five times b) about once a month c) more than once a month

4. At work, you have a) a couple of friends b) almost no friends c) lots and lots of friends

5. You a) enjoy your job b) don't really love your job, but try to appear content c) don't love your job and are unafraid to let it be known

6. If you found out that someone was gossiping about you, you would be a) annoyed b) furious c) indifferent

7. You tell secrets a) often b) rarely, if ever c) sometimes

8. You are on a) one social networking website b) no social networking websites c) several social networking websites

9. You update your profile for social networking websites a) often b) sometimes c) rarely, if ever

10. You would describe your life as a) fairly chilled out b) a little dull at times c) dramatic

11. Circle all of the following things that you have discussed when gossiping about other people: a) breakups b) promiscuity c) infidelity d) laziness e) eating, drinking, or party habits

KEY

1. a) 1 b) 2 c) 3

2. a) 2 b) 3 c) 1

3. a) 1 b) 2 c) 3

4. a) 1 b) 2 c) 3

5. a) 1 b) 3 c) 2

6. a) 2 b) 3 c) 1

7. a) 3 b) 1 c) 2

8. a) 1 b) 2 c) 3

9. a) 3 b) 1 c) 2

10. a) 2 b) 1 c) 3

11. Add 3 points for each item circled.

Total ____

RESULTS

10–17 points

You are GOSSIP-FREE. You are totally, absolutely sure that your business is not grist for the rumor mill. You're not involved with anything scandalous, and you don't really know anyone who gossips. You're pretty open about your life, so people don't have to do a lot of guesswork. You also, as a rule, never gossip yourself. It's really rude to talk about people behind their backs.

18–25 points

You are OUT OF THE HEADLINES. Likely, this is how you prefer it. Your life isn't exactly filled with the hottest news. You keep to yourself a fair amount, and you don't invite a huge amount of drama. In addition, you don't make yourself a part of gossipy scenes, so people just don't think of you in that context. They respect you for being a little bit above the fray. You're self-assured enough that you can make decisions in your own interest, which is a trait that all great leaders possess.

26–33 points

You are GOSSIP FODDER. And why shouldn't people talk about you? You lead an interesting life. It's not that you're trying to show off, but sometimes funny, unique, bizarre, or amazing things happen to you—not every day, but often enough. You enjoy telling stories and talking about other people, and sometimes that leads to making fun of someone behind his or her back, even if it's good-natured. People probably do the same thing to you, which kind of irks you when you think about it, but ultimately isn't the biggest deal.

34–39 points
You are FRONT-PAGE NEWS. While the chatter isn't constant, you frequently find yourself in the middle of major social flare-ups. You have an exciting life and know lots of people. Social engagements are a big deal, and you take them seriously. If this means that people are going to sit around and speculate about how you live, so be it. It's worth the occasional judgment from someone else to be a person worth talking about.

40–45 points
You are THE TALK OF THE TOWN. You practically live your life to have stories to tell later. You're honest about your feelings and quick to act on them. You've made a few foes over the years, but it's worth not having to act as if you like them. Your love life has, at times, been a mess, but there are perfectly good reasons for that. Gossiping about others is one of the great pleasures in life, and you'll partake in it with enthusiasm. You're close with your work friends, and the office often feels like a rumor mill. If people are talking about you behind your back (and they probably are), that makes you pretty angry—but at least you can say that your life is interesting.

What Does Your Lending Style Say About You?

1. Which of the objects pictured below would you lend to your best friend? Mark an "x" next to these. Which would you lend to a neighbor you barely know? Mark a "check" next to these.

2. You have insurance **a)** just on the house and car **b)** on nothing **c)** on many things

3. When your nice clothes get worn-out, you **a)** give them to a thrift store **b)** hand them down to someone else **c)** let them sit in your closet

4. Expensive electronics that you once paid a lot for **a)** are piled up somewhere in your house—they'll have retro value someday **b)** have long since been thrown out **c)** will be thrown out once you get around to it

5. Your most expensive possession, other than a house or car, is **a)** kind of a burden for you **b)** also one of your favorite possessions **c)** something about which you feel more or less neutral

6. You buy things, like sugar and salt, in **a)** huge, bulk quantities **b)** normal amounts **c)** small amounts

7. You keep your most treasured possessions **a)** in a drawer **b)** in a closet **c)** on display

8. Your favorite possession is something that a) only has meaning to you b) might be interesting to other people c) just about anyone would love

9. Giving a friend or loved one something you already own as a present is a) an insult b) a normal thing to do c) a beautiful thing to do

10. Your favorite possessions remind you of a) friends or family b) events, such as sports c) wealth

11. When you think about things you've lent out and not gotten back, you feel a) indifferent b) angry c) wistful

KEY

1. Add 1 point for each "x" and 3 points for each "check."

2. a) 2 b) 3 c) 1

3. a) 2 b) 3 c) 1

4. a) 1 b) 3 c) 2

5. a) 3 b) 1 c) 2

6. a) 3 b) 2 c) 1

7. a) 2 b) 1 c) 3

8. a) 1 b) 2 c) 3

9. a) 1 b) 2 c) 3

10. a) 3 b) 2 c) 1

11. a) 3 b) 1 c) 2

Total _____

RESULTS

10–19 points
You are a HOARDER. You have a hard time getting rid of things, let alone lending them to people who might actually have a use for them. When it comes to cleaning out closets and other messy areas, you try to be aggressive, but end up keeping almost everything. Whether it is worth money or has sentimental value, everything seems like it's worth hanging on to. When you do lend things out, you usually ask to have them back by a specific date, and you remember and remind the person.

20–29 points

You are SELECTIVE. It's not that you don't want to lend things, but it has to be to the right person, and it can't be something you really, really care about. So you pick and choose your situations, occasionally saying no even when someone really wants to borrow something. If you only lend out a few things at a time, it's a lot easier to remember who has what, and to make sure you get it back.

30–40 points

You are GENEROUS. Your stuff is important, but not so important that you wouldn't do a favor for a friend in need—or even someone you don't know, if you're in a good mood. You sometimes hold on to material possessions a little longer than you need to, but you also make an occasional trip to the thrift store to pass on your clothes to people who can use them. When you lend things out and don't get them back, you might remember and ask the person—but not every time, and definitely not when it comes to trivial objects.

41–50 points

You are PHILANTHROPIC. You like to give, and give big. If people ask to borrow something, you'll often give it to them along with several other items they didn't even ask about. There are certain things you want back eventually, though even for most of those it's entirely possible that you'll end up forgetting anyway.

51–60 points

You are LAVISH. Things have no value to you, compared to friends. You like the stuff you own and make good use of it, but if someone else can get more out of it, you have no reservations about giving it away. When you want to reminisce, you can do it with the memories in your head. And you certainly aren't waiting for anything you own to become a collector's item. When you lend things out, you do it with the expectation that you'll never see them again, and that's just fine with you.

What Do Other People Respect Most About You?

1. You have been a groomsman or bridesmaid at a) one wedding b) no weddings c) more than one wedding

2. You get your hair cut a) once a month or more b) every couple of months c) maybe once a year

3. You organize a) a regular event at your house or elsewhere b) no regular events c) more than one regular event

4. At all times, you carry a) one grooming implement b) multiple grooming implements c) no grooming implements

5. You usually shop for clothes a) with several friends b) with one or two friends c) by yourself

6. You deliberately try to make people laugh a) all the time b) rarely, if ever c) sometimes

7. When it comes to photos of you and your friends, you have a) one picture hanging up in your home b) no pictures hanging up in your home c) multiple pictures hanging up in your home

8. You are the president or head of a) more than one organization or group b) exactly one organization or group c) no organization or group

9. You have received a raise or promotion a) in the last year or two b) never c) at some point in your life

10. You have won an employee-of-the-month or other work award a) never b) many times c) once or twice

11. Compared with your income three years ago, you a) make more money now b) make about the same amount now c) make less now

12. At work, you wear a) more casual clothes than most of your coworkers b) sharper clothes than most of your coworkers c) the same kind of clothes as your coworkers

13. At work, you laugh a) rarely, if ever b) often c) sometimes

14. You get in trouble for socializing with coworkers a) often b) sometimes c) rarely, if ever

15. You discuss work with friends a) sometimes b) rarely, if ever c) often

16. In your workplace, you feel a) uncomfortable b) pretty comfortable c) very comfortable

KEY

1. a) 2 b) 1 c) 3	**6.** a) 2 b) 1 c) 3	**12.** a) 3 b) 2 c) 1
2. a) 1 b) 2 c) 3	**7.** a) 1 b) 2 c) 3	**13.** a) 1 b) 3 c) 2
3. a) 2 b) 1 c) 3	**8.** a) 2 b) 3 c) 1	**14.** a) 3 b) 2 c) 1
4. a) 2 b) 1 c) 3	**9.** a) 2 b) 1 c) 3	**15.** a) 3 b) 1 c) 2
5. a) 1 b) 2 c) 3	**10.** a) 1 b) 2 c) 3	**16.** a) 1 b) 3 c) 2
	11. a) 2 b) 3 c) 1	Total _____

RESULTS

16–24 points

You are respected for YOUR LOOKS. Not only are you naturally attractive, but you also dress nicely and are well-groomed. People want to know your secrets—whether they say it or not. You are often purposely placed in situations where other people can get a glimpse of you, and you are often invited along when people want advice about clothes. You may also be fun and intelligent, but people of both sexes gravitate toward you primarily for physical reasons.

25–32 points
You are respected for YOUR PROFESSIONAL SKILLS. You are charismatic, in a slick kind of way. You are seen as a natural leader who can organize people and accomplish goals. You are generally moving up in the work world, and for good reason. People place a lot of trust in you when it comes to decision making. You are a good negotiator and extremely effective at being a diplomat.

33–40 points
You are respected for YOUR INTELLIGENCE. You are considered a whiz, and people often admire your sharp mind. You are a quick learner, well schooled in many different subjects, and clever to boot. People often wish they had as many facts at their disposal as you have. It makes you a strong conversationalist and a go-to reference when people want to settle a complicated question. But it's not only facts you're good at: you also have a special ability to analyze the world around you.

41–48 points
You are respected for YOUR PERSONALITY. You are charismatic, in a heart-warming kind of way. You make people laugh, and you are full of lively ideas. You are the glue that keeps friends together. At work, people often wish they could hang out with you rather than sit silently next to you in a cubicle. You smile and laugh often, and it rubs off on others. You might be good-looking, but people are a lot more interested in what you have to say than what you look like.

Chapter **3**: **YOU + LIFESTYLE**

What's the Best Pet for You?

1. Your romantic relationships and friendships tend to last
   a) several years b) six months or less c) about a year

2. In relationships, you tend to take a a) leadership role
   b) passive role c) laid-back role

3. You believe that a good relationship requires a) hard work
   b) mutual respect c) some independence

4. When hanging out with a friend or partner, you prefer to
   a) be active b) engage in low-energy entertainment c) talk

5. You most enjoy a) cuddling b) roughhousing c) having your
   own space

6. When a friend or partner puts on some music, you usually
   a) don't pay attention b) get annoyed c) get interested in what
   is playing

7. You live a) by yourself b) with roommates c) with a romantic
   partner

8. In your household, you take out the trash a) most of the time
   b) rarely, if ever c) sometimes

9. Your home has a) very little natural light b) some natural light
   c) tons of natural light

10. You spend a) 40 hours a week at work b) less than 40 hours
    a week at work c) more than 40 hours a week at work

11. You take trips a) rarely, if ever b) often c) sometimes

12. When traveling, you pack a) light b) heavy c) what is
    necessary, plus some

13. Circle all of the following things you've done in your life.
a) Lost your keys or wallet b) Forgotten the password to your email account c) Forgotten someone you promised to pick up in the car d) Broken something expensive in a store e) Misspelled your name on an important document

KEY

1. a) 3 b) 1 c) 2

2. a) 3 b) 2 c) 1

3. a) 3 b) 2 c) 1

4. a) 3 b) 2 c) 1

5. a) 2 b) 3 c) 1

6. a) 3 b) 1 c) 2

7. a) 1 b) 3 c) 2

8. a) 3 b) 1 c) 2

9. a) 1 b) 3 c) 2

10. a) 2 b) 3 c) 1

11. a) 3 b) 1 c) 2

12. a) 1 b) 3 c) 2

13. Add 1 point for each item circled.

Total _____

RESULTS

12–21 points
Your ideal pet is a TURTLE, FISH, or HAMSTER. Considering your lifestyle and level of responsibility, you are best suited to an animal that can be left alone or cared for easily by another person. You would get along very well with an animal that stays out of the way.

22–31 points
Your ideal pet is a CAT. Like a feline, you prefer somewhat close relationships, but you also have a strong independent streak. You are responsible and caring enough to provide for the basic needs of a cat. You enjoy a little physical contact, but prefer some chilled-out petting to the kind of physical play typical with a dog.

32–41 points
Your ideal pet is a DOG. You would thrive on the intimacy and dependency of a canine. You don't mind being the leader in your relationships, and dogs give you that opportunity. Your tendency to form close and lasting friendships is totally consistent with a dog's sense of loyalty.

Which International Metropolis Suits You Best?

1. While at work, you communicate with your friends **a)** rarely, if ever **b)** sometimes **c)** perpetually

2. Changing careers is something you **a)** have considered **b)** can't imagine **c)** have done often

3. Your lunch break is **a)** an important way to break up your day **b)** taken at your computer **c)** nonexistent

4. You work **a)** for as many hours as you can stay awake **b)** for as few hours as possible **c)** pretty long hours

5. On the way home from work, you most want to **a)** sleep **b)** stop at the market to pick up groceries for dinner **c)** solve a crossword puzzle

6. Before going out, you spend **a)** five to ten minutes getting ready **b)** more than ten minutes getting ready **c)** no time getting ready—you usually go straight from work

7. The perfect garden is **a)** angular and well-maintained **b)** filled with secret spots **c)** in perfect balance with nature

8. You are most in awe when you see **a)** very old things **b)** very big things **c)** very new things

9. The fashion industry is **a)** too ostentatious **b)** extremely serious **c)** silly, but fun

10. Bars should be **a)** bright and filled with food **b)** stylish and filled with beautiful people **c)** dark and filled with sports fans

11. When a friend is late to pick you up, you **a)** let yourself get more and more impatient **b)** sit and watch whatever is happening around you **c)** try to do some work, if possible

12. You expect **a)** machines to compensate for human imperfection **b)** people to compensate for mechanical imperfection **c)** a little of both

13. Sporting events **a)** are most fun when they're all-day events **b)** should be two- or three-hour affairs, unless they go into overtime **c)** should be strictly timed

14. Mass transit should **a)** be an interesting place to see people **b)** move as many riders as quickly as possible **c)** have a historic feel

15. You prefer to take a stroll **a)** along a lovely river **b)** through a huge mall **c)** along historic streets

KEY

1. a) 3 b) 2 c) 1	**6.** a) 2 b) 1 c) 3	**12.** a) 3 b) 1 c) 2
2. a) 2 b) 1 c) 3	**7.** a) 1 b) 2 c) 3	**13.** a) 2 b) 1 c) 3
3. a) 2 b) 1 c) 3	**8.** a) 2 b) 1 c) 3	**14.** a) 1 b) 3 c) 2
4. a) 3 b) 2 c) 1	**9.** a) 3 b) 2 c) 1	**15.** a) 1 b) 3 c) 2
5. a) 3 b) 2 c) 1	**10.** a) 3 b) 1 c) 2	
	11. a) 1 b) 2 c) 3	Total ____

RESULTS

15–22 points
Your ideal metropolis is NEW YORK. Your no-nonsense attitude and social nature suggest that you would thrive in the Big Apple, where things are always moving and something is always happening. You don't mind working hard, as long as you can also do plenty of partying. You stand in awe of skyscrapers, and you don't mind living

➡

in tight quarters with 8 million people. After all, that's 8 million interesting stories.

23–30 points
Your ideal metropolis is PARIS. Your sophistication and fashion sense should make you feel right at home in France's capital. (And the food isn't bad either!) Life is too short to spend it working—you're much happier taking things a little slower. You love the most beautiful products of European culture, including museums, architecture, and music. You appreciate orderliness, but you don't want to be shoved in with countless other people every time you want to go somewhere.

31–37 points
Your ideal metropolis is LONDON. You are smart and appreciate sophistication, but you don't put on airs. You're happiest in a place that feels comfortable rather than overbearing. You appreciate a combination of modern art and classic buildings, and your idea of a perfect day is sitting in the sun during a cricket match, downing pints with your friends. In terms of your environment, coziness is much more important than good weather.

38–45 points
Your ideal metropolis is TOKYO. You are technologically savvy and look to human ingenuity to keep things ticking at an efficient pace. Cities should function according to the clock at all times. You are devoted to your work, far more than any other part of your life. Old buildings are nice, but they can't match the size and sleekness of more contemporary offerings. Your idea of a fun night is going out with coworkers after you clock out and getting in some quick karaoke, or taking care of some shopping in one place.

What's Your Decorating Style?

1. Circle all of the following patterns that you would wear on a prominent item of clothing.

   a) leopard print
   b) camouflage
   c) stripes
   d) argyle
   e) fleur-de-lis
   f) normal flowers

2. For a job interview, your clothes are a) crucial b) a hassle c) important, but only to the extent that you don't want to wear anything embarrassing

3. People should appreciate you for a) who you are as a person b) how hard you work c) your value as a friend

4. When posing for a photograph, you a) ham it up b) try to smile c) try to look mysterious

5. It is best to be a) respected b) loved c) ignored

6. The people who really matter in life are a) family b) friends c) the ones who can pull some strings for you

7. The most important object in your house for entertaining is the a) couch b) dining room table c) TV

8. When meeting a friend for dinner, you're most likely to suggest a) someplace new and unique b) a diner that serves good food c) whatever you know the other person likes

9. Home decoration is all about making the walls a) look less harsh b) interesting c) match the furniture

10. On Saturday morning, you'll check out a garage sale if you think you might be able to find **a)** some funny old junk **b)** something valuable amid the trash **c)** something useful

11. Spontaneity is **a)** a little frightening **b)** the spice of life **c)** so last year

KEY

1. a) 1 b) 1 c) 2
   d) 3 e) 3 f) 2

2. a) 3 b) 1 c) 2

3. a) 2 b) 3 c) 1

4. a) 1 b) 2 c) 3

5. a) 3 b) 1 c) 2

6. a) 2 b) 1 c) 3

7. a) 1 b) 3 c) 2

8. a) 3 b) 1 c) 2

9. a) 2 b) 1 c) 3

10. a) 1 b) 3 c) 2

11. a) 2 b) 1 c) 3

Total _____

RESULTS

10–15 points
Your decorating style is ADVENTUROUS. Your first priority with decoration is taking risks and seeking what excites. You're not afraid to experiment. It's worth pushing a few buttons in pursuit of making your home look not just good but spectacular!

16–21 points
Your decorating style is PLAYFUL. Everything in life can be viewed from another angle, and your goal is to seek out those angles. You like to experiment, joke, and make things more fun in general. You'd rather dress differently, talk differently, and be different—not because you're contrarian, but just because it adds a little something fresh. You decorate in ways that you think will make other people laugh feel good.

22–28 points

Your decorating style is LOW-KEY. For the most part, you prefer to keep your head down. You have a small, close group of friends, and you don't open up to many people beyond them. You may be closer with your family than with anyone else. You see no reason to express your opinions through your home by decorating in outlandish ways. You rarely try to make a strong impression, and instead try to manage your own affairs as best you can without help.

29–35 points

Your decorating style is TRADITIONAL. You feel like there is a right and wrong way to decorate. You seek out a style that might be described as "classic," paying respect to great designs of the past. You are drawn to sturdy material such as wood, rather than modern stuff such as stainless steel.

36–42 points

Your decorating style is HIGHBROW. You have champagne taste in many things, and you are constantly on the lookout for classy style flourishes that can augment your home. You hope that people will be awed by your taste and incredible eye. You not only want to make an impression, you want to wow people. Hanging out is an opportunity to entertain, lavishly when possible. Your home is designed expressly with visitors in mind.

What Does Your Ideal Night Out Reveal About You?

1. You are most likely to begin planning a night out a) a day or so in advance b) more than a day in advance c) a few hours or less in advance

2. The communication medium you are most likely to use when making plans is a) text message or email b) the telephone c) face-to-face

3. If you have to buy tickets or make a reservation, you prefer to do it a) at the door b) well in advance c) by asking someone to get you on the guest list

4. You think about your outfit a) rarely, if ever b) just before going out c) before you even know what you're going to do

5. You a) know exactly when you'll get home b) have absolutely no idea when you'll get home c) have an idea of when you'll get home, but are flexible

6. Getting the right group of people together for a night out involves a) careful forethought as to chemistry b) good luck c) having enough people so everyone can talk to someone

7. Conversation a) is key to a good night out b) can sometimes get awkward, so it's best to have something else to focus on c) requires just the right atmosphere

8. If you're hanging out with someone you don't like, a) the night is essentially ruined b) you just don't pay attention to the person c) it's a drag, but you just try to deal with it

9. Going out is a great chance to a) gossip b) get away from gossip

10. Adding someone to your group when you go out is **a)** fine—the bigger the party, the better! **b)** pretty awkward, usually **c)** OK, as long as the person can keep up

11. Everything is more entertaining when you **a)** have had a drink **b)** are with someone you love **c)** can share witty comments

12. When you're out on the town, you want the music to **a)** be the center of attention **b)** make everything more exciting **c)** be a pleasant sound track to whatever else you're doing

13. You most want to be entertained by **a)** the person or people you're with **b)** some kind of big spectacle **c)** a great meal

14. When it comes to spending money, you **a)** would prefer to rein it in **b)** don't mind paying whatever it costs for a really fun night **c)** will probably lose track of what you've spent by the end anyway, so it's hard to say

15. A sporting event is most likely **a)** a great night out **b)** a dreadful night out **c)** an OK way to start a night out

KEY

1. a) 2 b) 1 c) 3

2. a) 3 b) 1 c) 2

3. a) 2 b) 1 c) 3

4. a) 2 b) 1 c) 3

5. a) 1 b) 3 c) 2

6. a) 2 b) 1 c) 3

7. a) 2 b) 3 c) 1

8. a) 1 b) 3 c) 2

9. a) 1 b) 3

10. a) 3 b) 1 c) 2

11. a) 3 b) 1 c) 2

12. a) 1 b) 3 c) 2

13. a) 2 b) 3 c) 1

14. a) 2 b) 1 c) 3

15. a) 1 b) 2 c) 3

Total ____

RESULTS

15–25 points
Your ideal night out involves DINNER AND A MOVIE. You gravitate toward intimate situations and prefer to be in control. Situations with many variables can become stressful for you, so you try to plan things to a T and select activities that you understand well. Although you prefer the company of people you know to meeting strangers (even those who could become friends), you like to have specific activities planned so there isn't too much pressure on anyone. For these reasons, your ideal night out will usually end early.

26–34 points
Your ideal night out involves DRINKS WITH A GROUP OF FRIENDS. You have a pronounced social side, which really comes out when you're relaxing. You don't feel like you need much of a plan at all—in fact, too much ambition can spoil the time that friends get to spend together. You often feel like people have lost the art of conversation, and you work to try to bring it back. If you laugh a lot over the course of a night, that means the evening has been a success.

35–45 points
Your ideal night out involves DANCING AND WHO KNOWS WHAT ELSE? You are very social—almost aggressively so. In your opinion, a long night with lots of unexpected twists and outlandish stories is cathartic and pleasurable. You don't mind going places that are a little loud—you can always move on to another location if things get repetitive. This reflects a playful side in your personality, even though it also suggests that you may be impatient at times.

What Kind of Multi-Millionaire Would You Be?

1. Your savings account **a)** often falls down to zero dollars **b)** never falls down to zero dollars **c)** has fallen down to zero dollars in the past, but not often

2. You mostly pay for things **a)** with cash **b)** with a credit card **c)** with checks

3. When your paycheck arrives, you **a)** put it in your account and feel happy about your earnings **b)** immediately spend it on things you really need **c)** immediately spend it on things you really want

4. You do your taxes **a)** more or less on time **b)** late, at least some years **c)** well before the deadline

5. As a kid, you **a)** had your own bank account **b)** had a piggy bank that you raided after years of collecting change **c)** had a piggy bank that you raided all the time

6. You eat out at restaurants **a)** as often as you can **b)** rarely, if ever **c)** mostly when you don't have time to cook

7. The best entrée is **a)** the perfect sandwich **b)** a big, juicy porterhouse **c)** something starch-based, such as pasta

8. You do the dishes **a)** a few hours after cooking, or the next day **b)** at some point down the line **c)** immediately after cooking

9. You cook for others **a)** all the time **b)** rarely, if ever **c)** occasionally

10. When you see a great meal being cooked on TV, you **a)** try to find the ingredients as soon as you can **b)** find a restaurant that makes something similar **c)** feel bad about being a lousy cook

11. On airplanes, first class is **a)** really, really expensive **b)** actually kind of worth it, on some flights **c)** for people who think they're more important than they are

12. When you have a two-week vacation, you most want to **a)** see friends **b)** go somewhere interesting **c)** take a few days and just relax

13. You pack **a)** light **b)** heavy **c)** what is necessary, plus some

14. You take pets with you when you travel **a)** sometimes **b)** at all times **c)** rarely, if ever

15. You buy souvenirs from your trips **a)** rarely, if ever **b)** usually, mostly for yourself **c)** usually, mostly for friends

KEY

1. a) 3 b) 1 c) 2

2. a) 3 b) 2 c) 1

3. a) 2 b) 1 c) 3

4. a) 2 b) 3 c) 1

5. a) 1 b) 2 c) 3

6. a) 3 b) 1 c) 2

7. a) 2 b) 3 c) 1

8. a) 2 b) 3 c) 1

9. a) 3 b) 1 c) 2

10. a) 2 b) 3 c) 1

11. a) 3 b) 2 c) 1

12. a) 1 b) 3 c) 2

13. a) 1 b) 3 c) 2

14. a) 2 b) 3 c) 1

15. a) 2 b) 3 c) 1

Total ____

RESULTS

15–20 points

As a multi-millionaire, you would keep a LOW PROFILE. You have a history of being responsible with money, and while you may appreciate the finer things, you don't overindulge. No matter how much money you had stored away, you would be careful to keep it invested safely—things change, and you can never be too prepared. You are too aware of what really matters in life to let yourself get swept away in the desire to show off.

21–26 points
As a multi-millionaire, you would be QUIETLY CHARITABLE. You would spend a little, but not to make yourself look good. You would prefer to endow a local library or help a cause close to your heart. And you wouldn't need a plaque in your name either—if you've got a lot, it's only fair to spread it around.

27–33 points
As a multi-millionaire, you would be SOMEWHAT FLASHY. You are disciplined enough to hang on to your money, but by no means are you afraid to flash that gold watch while you roll with the windows down in your brand-new BMW. In fact, letting people know that you're among the elite is part of what keeps you in a position of respect. Besides, you would want to treat the people around you well—they deserve it.

34–39 points
As a multi-millionaire, you would be FREE-SPENDING. You might not spend all your money right away, but it will be hard to hang on to it for too long. You have a long mental list of things you would definitely get right away—house, car, clothes—and you'll be cutting generous checks for everyone in your life who has ever been good to you. You would try to put a little away, but you would devote yourself to spending pretty much full time.

40–45 points
As a multi-millionaire, you would be TOTALLY EXTRAVAGANT. You take risks and expect the world. You will gladly trade a little cash for greater convenience, even now; so just imagine what you'd be willing to pay for when you're wealthy. You want to invest just enough so you can keep living your lifestyle. Besides, spending on yourself is its own kind of investment. You have a "carpe diem" attitude—might as well spend the money while you've got it in your pocket!

What Do Your Favorite Foods Say About You?

1. For more flavor, you are most likely to add a little **a)** chili sauce **b)** Tabasco sauce **c)** black pepper

2. You are most likely to order **a)** mild salsa **b)** spicy salsa **c)** mango salsa

3. The little peppers next to items on a menu are useful **a)** indicators **b)** warnings **c)** enticements

4. When cooking with spices, you follow **a)** the recipe, to a T **b)** your tastebuds **c)** the recipe, more or less

5. You prefer **a)** rice **b)** pasta **c)** another grain or starch

6. No meal is complete without **a)** a cut of meat at the center **b)** an appetizer **c)** dessert

7. Side dishes **a)** should primarily complement the main course **b)** should just taste good **c)** aren't that important to a meal

8. You enjoy entrées that **a)** you already know you love **b)** give you a taste of something totally new **c)** feature a traditional dish done exceptionally well

9. Fried food is **a)** too heavy **b)** the most delicious **c)** good, sometimes

10. Baked food is **a)** boring **b)** often really great, but it depends on the dish **c)** nice and healthy

11. When you cook, you use **a)** a suitable amount of dishes, depending on your needs **b)** lots and lots of dishes **c)** as few dishes as possible

12. When ordering off a menu, it usually takes you **a)** about thirty seconds **b)** as long as several minutes **c)** no time at all—you usually know before you even look

13. Your choice of place setting **a)** is a full set for every meal **b)** depends on what you're eating at a given meal **c)** means grabbing a fork

14. When it comes to extra spices, you set out **a)** lots of them for guests to use **b)** salt and pepper **c)** none—the meal is good as it is

15. Garnish is **a)** key to making a meal look nice **b)** sometimes nice, but not at all important **c)** wasteful

16. Lighting in the room where you eat **a)** is totally unimportant **b)** is worth thinking about **c)** the lights should be on, that's all

KEY

1. a) 3 b) 2 c) 1	**6.** a) 1 b) 3 c) 2	**12.** a) 2 b) 3 c) 1
2. a) 1 b) 3 c) 2	**7.** a) 3 b) 2 c) 1	**13.** a) 2 b) 3 c) 1
3. a) 2 b) 1 c) 3	**8.** a) 1 b) 3 c) 2	**14.** a) 3 b) 1 c) 2
4. a) 1 b) 3 c) 2	**9.** a) 1 b) 2 c) 3	**15.** a) 2 b) 3 c) 1
5. a) 2 b) 1 c) 3	**10.** a) 1 b) 3 c) 2	**16.** a) 1 b) 3 c) 2
	11. a) 2 b) 3 c) 1	Total _____

RESULTS

16–26 points
You are CAUTIOUS. Convention gives you a safe footing, and you appreciate that. There are some things worth trying, but you know yourself pretty well at this point, and it often isn't worth the trouble of feeling awkward just for the sake of saying you did something unusual. It's not that you aren't willing to change, just that you won't do so without a lot of careful consideration. Change should happen slowly and deliberately, and it usually isn't worth a lot of risk.

27–37 points
You LIKE TO TRY NEW THINGS. You have a keen curiosity about the world around you, and when you spot something new and unique, you're usually game to try it. You don't jump in with both feet right away, but you try to arrange situations where you can dabble comfortably. You may have a mental list of experiences you'd like to have at some point.

38–48 points
You are VERY ADVENTUROUS. You really enjoy experimentation and consider yourself an open person. Possibilities should also be kept open, for the sake of fun if nothing else. The only thing holding you back from new experiences is usually opportunity—and when opportunity arises, you don't miss it. You are proud of the unusual things you've done, and you look forward to doing more. In the meantime, you don't mind a little risk.

Do You Spend Too Much Time Online?

1. On your favorite social networking site, you have **a)** one to three hundred friends **b)** zero friends—you're not on a social networking site **c)** more than three hundred friends

2. Through an online forum, you have **a)** many friends, even if you haven't met them in person **b)** just a couple friends **c)** no friends

3. Your closest friends spend **a)** about as much time online as you **b)** an obscene amount of time online **c)** not much time online

4. You provide status updates, in one place or another, **a)** many times a day **b)** rarely, if ever **c)** just once in a while

5. You tend to make social arrangements **a)** by email **b)** through a blog or social networking site **c)** in person or on the phone

6. You have **a)** a website or blog you update daily **b)** no website or blog, or one you update rarely **c)** a website or blog you update more than once a day

7. Your job requires you to be on the Internet **a)** all day long **b)** rarely, if ever **c)** from time to time

8. You take care of paying **a)** some bills online **b)** all bills online **c)** no bills online

9. At work, your email is open **a)** perpetually **b)** rarely, if ever **c)** sometimes

10. When you get a new message, you **a)** check it eventually **b)** read it along with several others, which you let accumulate for a few hours **c)** check it ASAP

11. You read the news **a)** mostly or entirely online **b)** in a newspaper **c)** rarely, if ever

12. When looking to buy used items, you first think about **a)** online auction sites **b)** thrift stores **c)** online classifieds sites

13. You have **a)** two or three websites you check every day **b)** more than three sites you check every day **c)** no sites you check every day

14. If you're eating alone, you're most likely to do it **a)** with a book or newspaper **b)** sitting in front of the TV **c)** sitting in front of the computer

15. When you can't get online, you **a)** often have more fun, actually **b)** have a somewhat hard time being entertained **c)** can't stop thinking about things you want to do once you get Internet access

KEY

	6. a) 2 b) 1 c) 3	**12.** a) 2 b) 1 c) 3
1. a) 2 b) 1 c) 3	**7.** a) 3 b) 1 c) 2	**13.** a) 2 b) 3 c) 1
2. a) 3 b) 2 c) 1	**8.** a) 2 b) 3 c) 1	**14.** a) 1 b) 2 c) 3
3. a) 2 b) 1 c) 3	**9.** a) 3 b) 1 c) 2	**15.** a) 1 b) 2 c) 3
4. a) 3 b) 1 c) 2	**10.** a) 2 b) 1 c) 3	
5. a) 2 b) 3 c) 1	**11.** a) 3 b) 1 c) 2	Total ____

RESULTS

15–20 points
You are INTERNET-AVERSE. Whether you didn't grow up with computers or you just don't like them, the Internet isn't a part of your life. All those strange words and technologies are totally confusing

when you read about them, and to tell the truth, you don't care one way or the other. Spending too much time online really isn't an issue for you.

21–26 points

You are a CASUAL WEB BROWSER. You may use the Internet as a resource but aren't too sucked in by it. You may be more suspicious or nervous about it than you need to be, but on the plus side, you aren't glued to a monitor twelve hours a day. You value your independence from a machine that can be a total time sink.

27–33 points

You are a DAILY SURFER. You take advantage of the Internet a lot, both at home and at your job. It makes many things more convenient, from shopping to communication to learning about current events. Plus, you like to be able to speak your mind to an audience sometimes. Still, you make a point of not overindulging—there are things in the world that don't require being plugged in.

34–39 points

You are CYBER-OBSESSED. You are an admitted Internet junkie. It often seems like every aspect of your life is mediated, in big ways, by a computer with a blazing-fast Internet connection. The Internet is entertaining, informative, and just plain necessary. You're not sure how you would survive without it. While you might, at times, wish you were less dependent on the Internet, it's basically impossible for you to log off!

40–45 points

You are a WEB ADDICT. You are beyond the point of being online too much—from morning until evening, you're online absolutely always. If you need to go somewhere away from home, you have a phone that gets Internet. So no matter where you are, you can work, socialize, and stay up-to-date. Even brief moments away from the Internet—in the shower, for example—can become stressful for you.

What Does Your Voice Tell Others?

1. Your voice sounds **a)** smooth **b)** raspy **c)** somewhere in-between

2. Your voice is **a)** somewhat nasal **b)** very nasal **c)** not at all nasal

3. Your voice is especially **a)** masculine **b)** feminine **c)** nondescript

4. Your singing voice is **a)** very nice! **b)** embarrassing **c)** OK—you don't sing often, so it's hard to say

5. When you want to sound angry, you **a)** bellow **b)** sound convincingly mad **c)** have a hard time sounding like you're serious

6. People tell you that you have a strong accent **a)** rarely, if ever **b)** sometimes **c)** all the time

7. When you are around your family, you **a)** find yourself talking like them **b)** find yourself saying a few words like them **c)** don't adapt to their accents at all

8. When speaking to someone important, you **a)** are aware of any accent you might have, but don't modify your speech much **b)** try to reduce any accent you might have **c)** don't think about your voice at all

9. When you get angry, you tend to **a)** scream **b)** raise your voice a little **c)** speak in your normal tone, just a little more sternly

10. You find others' accents to be **a)** sexy or intriguing **b)** hard to understand **c)** neutral

11. You use filler words such as "like" or "um" **a)** all the time **b)** not too often **c)** sometimes

12. You pause in the middle of sentences **a)** rarely, if ever **b)** often **c)** sometimes

13. You speak **a)** slowly **b)** at a normal pace **c)** quickly

14. You clear your throat **a)** sometimes **b)** not too often **c)** often

15. You **a)** are very good at imitations **b)** can do a few imitations **c)** can't do imitations at all

KEY

	6. a) 3 b) 1 c) 2	**12.** a) 1 b) 3 c) 2
1. a) 3 b) 1 c) 2	**7.** a) 3 b) 2 c) 1	**13.** a) 1 b) 2 c) 3
2. a) 2 b) 3 c) 1	**8.** a) 2 b) 3 c) 1	**14.** a) 2 b) 1 c) 3
3. a) 3 b) 3 c) 2	**9.** a) 3 b) 1 c) 2	**15.** a) 3 b) 2 c) 1
4. a) 1 b) 3 c) 2	**10.** a) 2 b) 3 c) 1	
5. a) 3 b) 2 c) 1	**11.** a) 3 b) 1 c) 2	Total ____

RESULTS

15–25 points
Your voice reveals that you are VERY RELAXED. You are even-keeled and good-tempered. You think about things before you speak, and you are intuitively skilled at keeping conversations going. Your voice has a pleasing sound, which stems from your comfort with yourself.

26–34 points
Your voice reveals that you are FAIRLY EVEN-TEMPERED. Your voice is pleasant for others to listen to, and yet you have the ability to let it be known when you are very happy or very upset, making you an excellent communicator.

35–45 points
Your voice reveals that you are HIGHLY EMOTIONAL. You have very little self-control when you feel elated or disappointed. Your voice has many different registers, which you make frequent use of. You do find yourself laughing often.

How Do You Overindulge?

1. Circle all of the following that you do *once a month or more*.
   a) Watch TV or go online while talking on the phone with a relative or friend **b)** Cheat on a diet **c)** Do work or study after midnight **d)** Buy something a little too expensive, just because **e)** Feel a strong sense of competition with a classmate or coworker

2. You eat dessert **a)** after dinner **b)** when you're feeling anxious **c)** rarely

3. Pleasurable things are best when **a)** you can do them all the time **b)** they're saved for special occasions **c)** you do them as often as you feel like doing them

4. When you find a song you really like, you **a)** listen to it constantly, until the novelty wears off **b)** listen to it just often enough that you can continue enjoying it **c)** play it for all your friends

5. When you receive awards or recognition, you feel **a)** gratified **b)** a little embarrassed at being the center of attention **c)** really filled up inside

6. The best meals are **a)** always those you make yourself **b)** usually the richest and heaviest **c)** the ones that someone else cooks

7. When you're sitting in the doctor's office waiting room, you **a)** read a magazine **b)** make plans in your head **c)** eat

8. A lazy Sunday is great for **a)** catching up with yard work or house chores **b)** sitting on the couch and relaxing **c)** going shopping

9. When you're by yourself on a long car ride, you're likely to
a) find a good radio station and stay there b) keep flipping
through the dial c) make a few phone calls on your cell phone

10. When you're just about done working for the day, you a) try to
think about whether there's any more work you can do before
actually going home b) plan to head straight home c) plan to
pick up a snack

11. When you're accompanying someone to the mall, you're most
likely to a) stare into space while the other person shops
b) give the other person advice on what to buy c) think of
something you want to buy, too, and shop for it

KEY

1. a) 1 b) 2 c) 3
d) 2 e) 3

2. a) 3 b) 2 c) 1

3. a) 1 b) 3 c) 2

4. a) 1 b) 2 c) 3

5. a) 1 b) 2 c) 3

6. a) 3 b) 2 c) 1

7. a) 1 b) 3 c) 2

8. a) 3 b) 1 c) 2

9. a) 1 b) 2 c) 3

10. a) 3 b) 1 c) 2

11. a) 1 b) 3 c) 2

Total ____

RESULTS

10–17 points
You are HIGHLY DISCIPLINED and don't overindulge. You have
incredible self-control, and you manage your life very well. You
recognize that balance is a positive thing, and you're able to avoid
doing things just because they feel good too often—even the best
things in life are less fun if you overindulge in them. You are patient
and restrained.

18–25 points

You overindulge in DISTRACTION. You let yourself zone out when conversations or events don't directly pertain to you. While this can be a handy trick in truly boring moments, you also miss a lot of detail by retreating into your own head. You can learn things you don't expect by keeping your mental antenna up more often.

26–33 points

You overindulge in IMMEDIATE GRATIFICATION. You are a sucker for satisfaction, and you look for it in passing pleasures. You think about what will make you feel good right now, rather than what might make you happiest in the long run. You can be impatient, and you may find yourself regretting some or many of your actions. Try to think of your "future self" as deserving of respect, too, to help your "current self" show a little more restraint.

34–41 points

You overindulge in ACTS OF SELF-IMPORTANCE. You have a soft spot for compliments, and sometimes fish for them. You can't get enough of being told that you're smart, talented, or attractive. This drive, at times, pushes you to work very hard so that others will really recognize your achievements. This is a type of overindulgence that can threaten your sense of satisfaction in life—try to be aware when you're going too heavy on it!

Which of the Five Senses Is Most Essential to You?

1. Which of the following applies to you? Answer yes or no.
   a) You wear glasses or contacts with a strong prescription.
   _____ b) You often smell produce to see if it might be spoiled. _____ c) You enjoy studying charts and graphs (at least somewhat). _____ d) You prefer to listen to the news on the radio rather than read it in the paper. _____
   e) You often add salt, pepper, and other spices to your food at the table. _____

2. You listen to music loudly while walking or driving. a) often b) rarely, if ever c) sometimes

3. When it comes to navigating with maps, you are a) totally lost b) skilled enough c) a whiz

4. If someone asks you for directions, you mostly direct them in terms of a) streets b) landmarks c) stores

5. You worry about your car making unusual sounds a) rarely, if ever b) sometimes c) often

6. If a stranger photographed you walking down the street, you would feel a) annoyed b) indifferent c) flattered

7. The biggest advantage of live music is a) the volume b) the presence of the musicians c) the excitement of the crowd

8. Your favorite format for music is a) MP3s b) CDs c) vinyl records

9. When you listen to music, you are most often a) listening very closely b) engaged in some other activity, like cooking or cleaning c) relaxing with friends

10. Your favorite characteristic of a song is the a) melody b) rhythm c) timbre (the sound of the instruments)

11. You follow the personal lives of your favorite musicians a) closely b) sometimes c) rarely, if ever

12. You remember people's names a) very well b) fairly well c) very badly

13. Historical dates are a) easy to remember b) fairly difficult to remember c) extremely difficult to remember

14. As a student, you retain the most information by a) listening to someone talk b) doing something yourself c) reading

15. In your head, it is easiest to recall a) specific voices b) specific flavors c) specific faces

16. When reminiscing with friends or family, you prefer a) telling stories b) looking at photos c) watching old home movies

17. The best type of museum is a) modern b) classical c) no museum—you don't enjoy them

18. Your favorite type of art is a) photography b) painting c) sculpture

19. You prefer art in your house to be a) in the kitchen b) in the living room c) in the bedroom

20. Which of the following would you most likely describe as a work of art? a) A great meal b) A great video game c) A great movie

21. In your opinion, artists should try to create work that **a)** is new and unusual **b)** is exceptionally beautiful **c)** makes a political statement

KEY

1. a) yes, 1 point; no, 3 points
b) yes, 1 point; no, 3 points
c) yes, 3 points; no, 1 point
d) yes, 1 point; no, 3 points
e) yes, 1 point; no, 3 points

2. a) 3 **b)** 1 **c)** 2

3. a) 1 **b)** 2 **c)** 3

4. a) 3 **b)** 1 **c)** 2

5. a) 3 **b)** 1 **c)** 2

6. a) 2 **b)** 1 **c)** 3

7. a) 1 **b)** 3 **c)** 2

8. a) 2 **b)** 3 **c)** 1

9. a) 2 **b)** 3 **c)** 1

10. a) 3 **b)** 1 **c)** 2

11. a) 3 **b)** 2 **c)** 1

12. a) 2 **b)** 1 **c)** 3

13. a) 3 **b)** 2 **c)** 1

14. a) 2 **b)** 1 **c)** 3

15. a) 2 **b)** 1 **c)** 3

16. a) 2 **b)** 3 **c)** 1

17. a) 3 **b)** 1 **c)** 2

18. a) 3 **b)** 2 **c)** 1

19. a) 2 **b)** 3 **c)** 1

20. a) 2 **b)** 1 **c)** 3

21. a) 1 **b)** 3 **c)** 2

Total ____

RESULTS

25–35 points

You favor the sense of TOUCH. You engage with your environment very directly, and you prefer immediate contact. You believe in things most when you can hold them in your hand. You are highly attuned to physical texture and don't mind being near other people. When you listen to music, you tend to move with it.

36–45 points

You favor the sense of TASTE. You take great pleasure in eating, and there are few foods you're afraid of. Furthermore, when you eat, you tend to think very carefully about flavors, and you may well be a great chef yourself! You have an extremely hard time being around things that are inedible, like garbage.

46–55 points

You favor the sense of SMELL. Like people who favor taste, food is an important part of your life. But you also have a well-developed sense of smell in other areas. You are constantly noticing people's scents and are always the first to notice potential hazards like a gas leak from the stove.

56–65 points

You favor the sense of HEARING. You are excellent at gathering signals from sounds in the air, and you often find yourself relying on them as warnings about the world around you. When you listen to music, you are greatly affected by the texture of the sound—perhaps even more than by melody or rhythm. You greatly enjoy people who have beautiful voices, either for singing or speaking.

66–75 points

You favor the sense of SIGHT. You are highly analytical and rational, and you may be especially skilled at math or science. You demand to see things in order to understand them better, and you generally feel that things you can't see probably don't exist. You understand music and art as practical and pleasant, but tend not to feel them very strongly.

Chapter **4**: **YOU + CAREER**

What Are Your Strongest Talents?

1. Proofread the following memo. How many errors can you find?

To Who It May Concern in the Accounting Office,

Mr. Johnson wants a report on her desk by tomorrow morning regarding the Wilson project. He is concerned that we will lose one of our biggest clients if we dont act quickly. Mr. Johnson will be in the office by 8:00 a.m. sharp. The acounting office must be responsible for this material. Please do not neglect this It is very important.

Sincerely,

Wanda

2. You are most likely to **a)** organize a meeting **b)** fall asleep at a meeting **c)** think of an idea at a meeting

3. Meetings work best when they're **a)** short and sweet **b)** peppered with a little humor **c)** open to contribution from everyone

4. Agendas **a)** usually go out the window no matter what **b)** are very important **c)** are a pain in the neck

5. The main purpose of meetings is **a)** for management to yak **b)** for everyone in the office to see one another face-to-face **c)** to hash out specific ideas

6. An ideal meeting room would have **a)** really comfy chairs **b)** a projection screen so everyone can have their attention focused in one place **c)** a chalkboard for brainstorming

7. When assigned a new project, you usually **a)** grumble **b)** feign excitement **c)** feel flattered

8. When given an assignment, you **a)** do exactly what's asked **b)** try to consult with coworkers to get ideas **c)** try to add personal touches to the finished product

9. You prefer **a)** short projects you can finish quickly **b)** projects you can delve into for a while, but finish before you get bored **c)** long projects with an indefinite end date

10. When collaborating on projects with coworkers, you **a)** are somewhat interested in their input, but more in their talents **b)** often feel that things would go more smoothly if you were alone **c)** often get behind because of socializing

11. When working with someone below you in the hierarchy, you **a)** often get annoyed at your coworker's incompetence **b)** try really hard to teach the person something **c)** try to figure out what your coworker can contribute

KEY

1. For each error you found, add 3 points. **Errors: 1.** Salutation: "To Who**m** It May Concern" **2.** First sentence: "wants a report on **his** desk" **3.** Third sentence: "don**'t**" **4.** Fifth sentence "ac-**c**ounting" **5.** Sixth sentence: "Please do not neglect this."

2. a) 2 b) 3 c) 1

3. a) 3 b) 1 c) 2

4. a) 2 b) 3 c) 1

5. a) 1 b) 2 c) 3

6. a) 1 b) 3 c) 2

7. a) 3 b) 2 c) 1

8. a) 3 b) 2 c) 1

9. a) 2 b) 3 c) 1

10. a) 1 b) 3 c) 2

11. a) 3 b) 2 c) 1

Total _____

RESULTS

10–21 points
Your strongest talent in the workplace is CREATIVITY. Many thoughts crop up in the fertile corners of your mind. You constantly look for new angles that others have failed to consider. This makes you a tremendous asset for projects where a human touch can really impress people. While you may not be the most careful proofreader, and others might regard you as sometimes out of left field, when you hit on a good concept, it can make a big splash.

22–33 points
Your strongest talent in the workplace is NETWORKING. You understand that the most valuable skill in any work environment is making strong, trusting contacts between people. You pay attention to the way others talk to you, the way they shake hands, and much more. This makes you a great collaborator, both in your own workplace and when you interact with people outside of it. While you may not be the most concerned with spreadsheets or reports, you work hard to be a great face for your business.

34–45 points
Your strongest talents in the workplace are READING AND WRITING. You are clear-eyed and assiduous, and a disciplined employee. Your intelligence and training have given you a keen eye for detail, which makes written material much better for your having browsed it. You put a high premium on efficiency, and you get bored quickly with office politics and the like. Work is a very goal-oriented process, and you organize your tasks incredibly well.

What Line of Work Suits You Best?

1. You aspire to make **a)** just enough to support yourself **b)** as much as you possibly can **c)** enough to be quite comfortable

2. You prefer to be paid according to **a)** the amount of work you do **b)** the quality of work you do **c)** the number of hours of work you do

3. I prefer for work to **a)** have nothing to do with the rest of my life **b)** be the central passion of my life **c)** be somewhat involved with the rest of my life

4. Working late **a)** is good news—it means you're succeeding! **b)** is soul-sucking **c)** just comes with the territory

5. Working weekends is OK if **a)** it only happens on very rare occasions **b)** you're getting paid extra for it **c)** it's a true emergency

6. The best way to ensure job security is to **a)** do a fantastic job **b)** work in a field that's always hiring **c)** keep your head down and do what you're asked

7. Lunch should be **a)** long, and taken when you need it most **b)** a brief affair, if you do it at all **c)** taken at the exact same time every day

8. Having lots of vacation time is **a)** something you earn after years of dedication to a job **b)** necessary for your sanity **c)** necessary to keep your mind agile

9. You prefer for your coworkers to **a)** be partners, but not collaborators **b)** have their own specializations, different from yours **c)** be people who can inspire you

10. When you show up to work, you want **a)** to know exactly what you're doing before you arrive **b)** for the day to be a surprise **c)** to be able to respond to other people's needs as necessary

11. Loving your job is **a)** very important **b)** somewhat important **c)** not important

12. Having your job improve other people's lives is **a)** very important **b)** somewhat important **c)** not important

13. Having your job impress people is **a)** very important **b)** somewhat important **c)** not important

14. Having lots of free time to yourself is **a)** very important **b)** somewhat important **c)** not important

15. You want to retire **a)** as soon as you can **b)** late **c)** when you're dead

KEY

1. a) 3 b) 1 c) 2	**6.** a) 1 b) 2 c) 3	**12.** a) 2 b) 1 c) 3
2. a) 2 b) 1 c) 3	**7.** a) 1 b) 2 c) 3	**13.** a) 2 b) 1 c) 3
3. a) 3 b) 1 c) 2	**8.** a) 3 b) 2 c) 1	**14.** a) 3 b) 1 c) 2
4. a) 1 b) 3 c) 2	**9.** a) 2 b) 3 c) 1	**15.** a) 3 b) 2 c) 1
5. a) 3 b) 1 c) 2	**10.** a) 3 b) 1 c) 2	
	11. a) 1 b) 2 c) 3	Total ____

RESULTS

15–24 points
You are best suited for a career in THE ARTS, whether as a writer, painter, musician, or photographer. Although artistic jobs famously pay peanuts, if your talent is ever recognized, you could do fantastically well in the end. Besides, as an artist you get to express yourself through your work and potentially be your own boss as well. The combination of freedom and a big payday (if you're really good—and you think you might be) is enough to drive you toward a career in an artistic field.

25–35 points
You are best suited for a PROFESSIONAL OCCUPATION, whether as a doctor, teacher, accountant, or lawyer. You are smart, and you care about people very deeply. Professional jobs require a lot of training, the people you work with can be needy, and the hours can be long, but the feeling of doing good is enough to make it all worth it. You like the idea of having your own practice or classroom, where you can decide on the atmosphere and make it your own. And the money isn't bad, either.

36–45 points
You are best suited for an OFFICE ENVIRONMENT, perhaps as an administrator, IT technician, or bookkeeper. Work isn't really the central focus of your life. You might be more concerned about family, vacation time, or decent benefits. You've never been a terribly ambitious employee, and that's fine with you. You're consistent, you show up every day and put in your time, and then the rest of the day is yours.

What Grade Does Your Job Receive?

1. When you wake up in the morning, you **a)** dread going to work **b)** don't mind going to work **c)** love going to work

2. Mondays are **a)** just like every other day **b)** a real drag **c)** an exciting beginning

3. When it comes to vacation days, you **a)** figure out how to use them way ahead of time **b)** sometimes lose them at the end of the year, since you haven't taken them **c)** think about using them once they've accumulated

4. The end of the day usually comes **a)** as a surprise **b)** after a lot of looking at the clock **c)** about when you expect it

5. When someone asks you to do something, you **a)** have often already done it **b)** usually offer excuses **c)** do it

6. Your boss **a)** does his or her job well enough **b)** is a joke **c)** is an inspiration

7. You join after-work activities **a)** often **b)** sometimes **c)** rarely, if ever

8. You have made **a)** a good friend from among your coworkers **b)** many good friends from among your coworkers **c)** no good friends at your job

9. You eat lunch with coworkers **a)** rarely, if ever **b)** often **c)** sometimes

10. You enjoy working closely with coworkers **a)** at times **b)** hardly ever **c)** very much

11. You came to your current job because **a)** it was a great opportunity **b)** it's actually your first job **c)** you lost a previous job

12. Your salary or hourly wage seems to **a)** be higher than similar jobs elsewhere **b)** be about the same as similar jobs elsewhere **c)** be less than at similar jobs elsewhere

13. Compared to staff at other workplaces, you and your colleagues seem to work **a)** more efficiently **b)** less efficiently **c)** about as well

14. The future of your company or organization is **a)** bright **b)** not likely to change much **c)** bleak

15. You think about putting in your two weeks' notice **a)** every day **b)** never **c)** only at extreme moments

KEY

	6. a) 2 b) 1 c) 3	**12.** a) 3 b) 2 c) 1
1. a) 1 b) 2 c) 3	**7.** a) 3 b) 2 c) 1	**13.** a) 3 b) 1 c) 2
2. a) 2 b) 1 c) 3	**8.** a) 2 b) 3 c) 1	**14.** a) 3 b) 2 c) 1
3. a) 1 b) 3 c) 2	**9.** a) 1 b) 3 c) 2	**15.** a) 1 b) 3 c) 2
4. a) 3 b) 1 c) 2	**10.** a) 2 b) 1 c) 3	
5. a) 3 b) 1 c) 2	**11.** a) 3 b) 2 c) 1	Total ____

RESULTS

15–20 points
Your job is rated F FOR FOUL, or run as FAST as you can! You are unmotivated, unfulfilled, and unexcited about your career track. You often feel stuck in a rut, and don't consider your superiors to be worthy of their places above you. If possible, you should think about taking practical steps to move on. This position just doesn't seem like the gig that's going to take you where you want to go.

21–26 points

Your job is rated D FOR DREADFUL. There clearly isn't much here for you, even if it sometimes feels like too much hassle to search for something else. All signs point to you feeling more and more unhappy as time goes on, and the compensation hardly makes it worthwhile. Get out now, before your bottled-up dissatisfaction boils over.

27–33 points

Your job is rated C FOR CONVENTIONAL. Like a lot of people, you punch the clock, do your work, and head home. You're not particularly stimulated by your work, but the general environment could be worse. If you're just looking to pay the bills, by all means stick around, but recognize that there may be better opportunities out there for you.

34–39 points

Your job is rated B FOR BENEFICIAL. Whether it's salary, personal satisfaction, or a great workplace, you're definitely getting something from your current job—but not all of these things at the same time. In other words, there are pros and cons in your work, and the pros might be reason enough to stay for now. But make sure to keep careful track of your satisfaction. Even a slight shift toward the cons could be reason enough to reconsider.

40–45 points

Your job is rated A FOR AMAZING. You enjoy the people around you, feel like you're working toward something important, and are satisfied with your pay. When you get up in the morning, you actually *want* to go in to work—count yourself lucky! You see lots of light at the end of the tunnel as far as staying with your current organization, and possibly even moving toward a position of greater responsibility. Congratulations!

What Does Your Workspace Publicize About You?

1. When it comes to pictures of friends and family, you have
a) a few b) tons c) none

2. When it comes to plants, you have a) a few b) some, but
they're in pretty bad shape c) none

3. When it comes to cartoons and jokey things hanging up, you
have a) none b) a wall full—or more! c) just a few

4. Office decorations are a) tacky b) cheerful c) just a way to
make things less dull

5. Your decorations a) are the same at all times b) change once
they get really stale c) change for the holidays!

6. Your workspace is a) spic-and-span b) a little cluttered
c) a frightening mess

7. When it comes to finding materials, you a) can do it in a minute,
b) can do it instantly c) often have to dig for a while

8. Food in the work area is a) just fine b) gross! c) OK, once in a while

9. Your computer files are a) in disarray b) superbly organized
c) more or less organized

10. Your coworkers a) can be as messy as they want b) should try
to be neater—their mess constantly gets in your way c) should
try to be courteous about their organization when possible

11. You hide your computer monitor a) very carefully b) only when
surfing the Web c) rarely, if ever

12. When it comes to private files on your computer, you a) have
none b) have a few, but don't protect them c) keep them in a
password-protected folder

13. You close your door **a)** sometimes **b)** rarely **c)** often

14. You tell your coworkers about the details of your work
a) all the time **b)** rarely, if ever **c)** if it comes up

15. You leave important documents around **a)** very often
b) rarely, if ever **c)** sometimes

KEY

1. a) 2 b) 3 c) 1
2. a) 3 b) 1 c) 2
3. a) 1 b) 3 c) 2
4. a) 1 b) 2 c) 3
5. a) 1 b) 2 c) 3

6. a) 3 b) 2 c) 1
7. a) 2 b) 3 c) 1
8. a) 1 b) 3 c) 2
9. a) 1 b) 3 c) 2
10. a) 1 b) 3 c) 2
11. a) 1 b) 2 c) 3

12. a) 2 b) 3 c) 1
13. a) 2 b) 3 c) 1
14. a) 3 b) 1 c) 2
15. a) 3 b) 1 c) 2

Total ____

RESULTS

15–24 points
You are a PRIVATE PERSON. This is not quite the same as being an organized person. In fact, the lack of clutter serves as a buffer against potential intruders nosing into your space and your life.

25–35 points
You are an OPEN PERSON. You like a little decoration in your work life. While you don't wear your heart on your sleeve, you are also not emotionally defensive. If a person proves to be a true friend, you will share almost anything.

36–45 points
You are a PEOPLE PERSON. You are very interested in the lives of other people, and attract them into your space with your décor. You may even be considered an office gossip. You are a friendly, considerate person, but you can sometimes overstep your bounds.

Are You a Great Coworker?

Imagine you are writing an important, but sensitive, email to a coworker who has the same job as you. From the choices given, circle the phrasing that you would most likely use in each sentence.

Thank you for taking care of writing that letter yesterday. I was swamped and couldn't get to it. I [**1. a)** will return the favor sometime **b)** will buy you a drink **c)** really appreciate it]. Unfortunately, I found a couple of [**2. a)** mistakes in **b)** problems with **c)** issues with] the letter. Some of the details need to be [**3. a)** reworked **b)** considered more carefully **c)** edited]. How about [**4. a)** we go over it together **b)** you look at it again and get back to me **c)** we ask another coworker for an opinion]? Anyway, thanks again, and [**5. a)** I'm sorry to be so negative **b)** I'll talk to you soon **c)** once again, I appreciate your effort].

Sincerely,

Me

6. When listening to music or the radio at work, you **a)** always use headphones **b)** never use headphones **c)** sometimes use headphones

7. When coworkers eat strong-smelling food at their desks, you **a)** don't notice **b)** sometimes get annoyed **c)** often get annoyed

8. You complain about the temperature of your workplace **a)** sometimes **b)** rarely, if ever **c)** every day

9. If you get a personal phone call at work, you **a)** take it **b)** go outside **c)** try to keep it short

10. Coworkers looking at non-work-related websites a) don't bother you b) bother you only if they go overboard c) bother you a lot

11. Looking over other people's work is a) useful for everyone b) useful for the person who needs help c) often not that productive

12. When your coworker is home sick, you a) fill in for your coworker b) let your coworker deal with her own darn work c) fill in, but only if you think the excuse is real

13. A group of coworkers are a) competing to climb a narrow ladder b) a team c) in the same boat, which might not always sail in the right direction

14. When it comes to your coworkers' workloads, you know a) a little b) almost nothing c) a lot

15. You are a go-to person for a) very few things b) many things, most of them minor c) many important things

KEY

1. a) 2 b) 1 c) 3
2. a) 3 b) 2 c) 1
3. a) 2 b) 1 c) 3
4. a) 3 b) 2 c) 1
5. a) 1 b) 2 c) 3
6. a) 2 b) 1 c) 3
7. a) 3 b) 2 c) 1
8. a) 2 b) 1 c) 3
9. a) 1 b) 3 c) 2
10. a) 2 b) 3 c) 1
11. a) 3 b) 2 c) 1
12. a) 3 b) 1 c) 2
13. a) 1 b) 2 c) 3
14. a) 3 b) 1 c) 2
15. a) 1 b) 2 c) 3

Total ____

RESULTS

15–22 points
You are an APATHETIC COWORKER. To put it bluntly, you're sort of a drag around the office. This doesn't mean you're a bad person—in fact, it may very well just be an indication that this job isn't for you. You avoid responsibility and effort whenever possible, which means that your coworkers have to work extra hard with you around, and that's not how it's supposed to be.

23–29 points
You are a MEDIOCRE COWORKER. You pitch in here and there, but you're mostly at the office for your own benefit. Your colleagues might like you a lot personally, but as a coworker, you're just OK. You don't put in a lot of effort to be helpful, and you don't try that hard to make the environment around you comfortable for everyone. You're not overly concerned about people's feelings, and not because you feel it's important to be honest.

30–37 points
You are a GOOD COWORKER. People look to you for advice and leadership, and they appreciate what you have to offer. While you're not a perfect model citizen in the office, you do make a good faith effort to share, pitch in, and be a mentor when necessary. Others like having you around—you give off good vibes!

38–45 points
You are a GREAT COWORKER! Congrats! You are happy, productive, and friendly—the kind of colleague everyone gravitates toward. You put others first almost always, and are highly skilled at bringing out the best in them. You are admired by your peers, by your superiors, and by those below you in the hierarchy—a rare feat! Everyone recognizes your talents, and they're drawn to your positive, constructive attitude.

Do You Spend Too Much Time at Work?

1. Circle all of the following that apply. I am at work **a)** when no one else is in the office for five or more hours a week **b)** after 10 p.m. two or more times per week **c)** while eating food five or more times week **d)** when I should be on holidays four or more times a year **e)** when I don't feel well enough to be there three or more times a year

2. You watch movies **a)** at least once a month **b)** at least once a week **c)** less than once a month

3. You cook a proper dinner **a)** about once a week **b)** less than once a week **c)** more than once a week

4. You eat breakfast sitting down **a)** every day **b)** a few days a week **c)** less than a few days a week

5. You visit friends out of town **a)** once in a while **b)** all the time **c)** almost never

6. At parties, work is **a)** a fine topic of conversation, for small talk, anyway **b)** the easiest thing to talk about, usually **c)** a terrible choice of conversation topic

7. You get about **a)** seven to nine hours of sleep a night **b)** six hours of sleep a night **c)** less than six hours of sleep a night

8. Outside work, you are most likely to check work email **a)** before you get to your workplace **b)** after you've gone home for the day **c)** rarely, if ever

9. Taking work with you on a vacation **a)** can be a great, surprisingly relaxing way to catch up **b)** is a depressing idea **c)** makes sense, as long as it's only a little bit of work

10. Your social circle talks about work a) rarely, if ever b) sometimes c) often

11. You dream or are kept awake at night thinking about work obligations a) every once in a while b) often c) rarely, if ever

KEY

1. Add 3 points for each answer marked.

2. a) 2 b) 1 c) 3

3. a) 2 b) 3 c) 1

4. a) 1 b) 2 c) 3

5. a) 2 b) 1 c) 3

6. a) 2 b) 3 c) 1

7. a) 1 b) 2 c) 3

8. a) 2 b) 3 c) 1

9. a) 1 b) 3 c) 2

10. a) 3 b) 2 c) 1

11. a) 2 b) 3 c) 1

Total ____

RESULTS

10–22 points
You're a SLACKER. You're in such a rush to head home that you may be neglecting basic responsibilities around the office. If people see that you're never around, they may question your commitment. It may be healthy to think about your job just a little bit when you aren't in the office. And be careful not to let your inbox pile up while you're off enjoying yourself.

23–30 points
You're a RELIABLE EMPLOYEE. You manage the fine art of keeping life and job separate, and you manage it well! You not only leave the office on time, but you don't carry that baggage with you when you leave. You stay psychologically separated from workplace issues when it's time to relax. You understand that you have an obligation not only to your boss, but also to your friends and family—as well as yourself.

30–37 points

You're an OVER-WORKER. While you know that it's bad for work to consume you, you'll sometimes stay a little longer than you should. You can't help it. Every once in a while, you might even be late for something you're supposed to do after work, because you needed to finish up a project or a conversation. You think about—and even do—work on the road or at home, sometimes wishing you weren't.

38–45 points

You're a WORK ADDICT. Not only are you physically at work for too long every day, but your mind is there almost all the time. Your work life provides not only income, but also the drama that sustains you. You constantly think about projects, coworkers, schedules, and much more. You're very likely have a portable device that helps you get tasks done when you're on the go. All of this adds up, and when you need a break, you need it badly. Be careful about this cycle—it isn't good for you.

If You Lived During the Renaissance, What Would Your Ideal Job Be?

In your free time, would you rather . . .

1. a) watch TV b) go for a walk

2. a) go to a museum b) do some work around the house

3. a) exercise b) sit on the beach

4. a) cook b) go to a restaurant

5. a) read the newspaper b) listen to music

6. When it comes to mechanical objects, you a) often wonder how they work b) sometimes wonder how they work c) don't much care *how* they work, as long as they work

7. When something you own breaks, you a) try to fix it, if you already know how b) throw it away c) always try to fix it

8. Science a) answers certain questions very well b) has the potential to tell us many new and exciting things about the universe c) is kind of boring

9. When it comes to activities you've never tried before, you a) usually jump right in b) might try, if it seems like it'll be worth it c) prefer to stay home

10. Your favorite reading material is a) informative b) beautiful c) no material—you don't read much

11. The best possessions are a) things you can display b) things you can enjoy using every day c) things that make your life easier

12. Your house is decorated with a) things you've made b) things you've collected c) practical objects, rather than beautiful ones

13. When something goes out of fashion, you a) usually don't notice b) get rid of it as soon as possible c) try to hang onto it a little while longer, so you at least get your money's worth

14. When you give presents, they will ideally a) come from the heart b) come from exotic places c) be useful for the recipient

15. Your possessions make you feel a) accomplished b) superior c) inspired

KEY

1. a) 5 b) 2
2. a) 4 b) 2
3. a) 3 b) 4
4. a) 1 b) 3
5. a) 2 a) 4
6. a) 1 b) 2 c) 3
7. a) 2 b) 3 c) 1
8. a) 2 b) 1 c) 3
9. a) 1 b) 3 c) 2
10. a) 1 b) 2 c) 3
11. a) 3 b) 1 c) 2
12. a) 1 b) 3 c) 2
13. a) 1 b) 3 c) 2
14. a) 2 b) 3 c) 1
15. a) 1 b) 3 c) 2

Total _____

RESULTS

20–27 points
Your ideal Renaissance job would be as an ALCHEMIST. You have an innate interest in things, and a desire to manipulate them. You crave new discoveries and new technologies, and you love understanding the

tricks that make them work. Finally, you strongly believe that there is always more on the horizon to learn, if we keep our eyes and ears open.

28–35 points

Your ideal Renaissance job would be as a CARPENTER. Like the alchemist, you enjoy getting your hands a little dirty. But you are more interested in creating beautiful things than in pure discovery. You have a keen aesthetic and love the feeling that comes from building something, especially if someone can put it to good use. You tinker a bit but believe that there is a right and wrong way to do everything.

36–43 points

Your ideal Renaissance job would be as a PAINTER. You believe in the concept of beauty, and feel that the way to make it emerge is through hard work and self-expression. The human form and the natural world are amazing things—the ultimate tribute is to be able to represent them artistically. You see art not as subversive, but as inspiring and universal.

44–50 points

Your ideal Renaissance "job" would be as ROYALTY. You have champagne tastes and little interest in using your hands. You are confident and self-aware, perhaps better suited to govern others than to do manual labor on your own. You like to collect things, and you require a good deal of flattery. A royal position would suit your personality perfectly.

What Do Your Retirement Aspirations Say About You?

1. You began (or will begin) saving money for retirement a) as soon as you started working full time b) around middle age c) waaayy too late

2. Your savings strategy for your golden years is a) pretty standard b) almost nonexistent c) carefully crafted

3. When you stop working, you expect to a) move somewhere sunny b) stay exactly where you are c) figure it out when the time comes

4. With more free time after retirement, you expect to a) spend more time with your family b) spend more time doing what you love c) get anxious about not having any work to do

5. As a retiree, you expect your time to be a) totally free b) very well-structured c) somewhat structured, but not too much

6. Which of the following do you think will appeal to you when you're retired? Mark each that applies. a) Buying a boat b) Writing a memoir c) Sleeping in d) Starting a foundation e) Sunbathing

7. You expect to leave your current job closest to age a) sixty-five b) fifty-five c) seventy-five

8. Your current employer gives you a) no retirement benefits b) great retirement benefits c) decent retirement benefits

9. On your last day of work, you want a) to leave quietly, without pomp and circumstance b) a big, fun party with your coworkers c) a big, fun party with your friends later on

10. If your company asked you to retire tomorrow, you would
a) gladly do so b) hold out as long as possible c) try to negotiate a nice retirement package

11. The odds that you will end up working again, in some capacity, after you formally retire are a) 50 percent b) 0 to 10 percent c) 80 to 100 percent

KEY

1. a) 3 b) 2 c) 1

2. a) 2 b) 1 c) 3

3. a) 1 b) 3 c) 2

4. a) 2 b) 1 c) 3

5. a) 1 b) 3 c) 2

6. a) 1 b) 3 c) 1
  d) 3 e) 1

7. a) 2 b) 1 c) 3

8. a) 1 b) 3 c) 2

9. a) 3 b) 2 c) 1

10. a) 1 b) 3 c) 2

11. a) 2 b) 1 c) 3

Total _____

RESULTS

10–18 points
You are a true PERSON OF LEISURE. Retirement feels like it was made for you because you are drawn to the good life. There is no such thing as too much time doing exactly what you want. You like the ideas of personal freedom and wide-open space. Your approach to retirement suggests that these exemplify your natural state. You are very good at relaxing and letting yourself feel loose.

19–25 points
You are a PERSON FOR ALL SEASONS. Your retirement aspirations suggest that you are highly adaptable. You can find satisfaction in anything you're doing, whether it's intense work or open-ended leisure time. One way or another, retirement will work for you. You rarely get

frustrated or feel trapped because you know you can always adjust your frame of mind.

26–32 points
You are DRIVEN. Many people wait their whole lives for retirement, but it makes you a little nervous. You just can't imagine your days without work as a form of structure. You would feel useless if you weren't accomplishing goals all of the time, and without the respect that comes along with doing so. Your entire career has been about new ideas and personal improvement, and you can't imagine sacrificing all that.

33–39 points
RETIREMENT? WHAT'S THAT? You've always figured that when your current career ends, you'd start another project—either a second career, a business, or some other big venture. The very idea of turning into a prune at some condo in Florida—not that there's anything wrong with that—never even occurred to you. As long as you're healthy, you plan to move full steam ahead. Besides, you have lots of business ideas saved up that you can't wait to try out.

How Far Will You Climb in Your Current Job?

1. When you go to a sporting event and your team is losing, you
   a) leave very early b) stick around for a while, but leave just
   early enough to beat the crowds c) stay all the way to the end

2. Your main goal in life is to a) support a family b) find happiness
   c) change the world

3. Being a leader requires a) the will to boss people around
   b) a clear vision c) charisma

4. Political idealism is a) noble, but not always practical b) silly
   c) always noble

5. Climbing a mountain is a) reckless b) an intriguing idea
   c) something you've already done

6. You have been at your current job for a) more than ten years
   b) between five and ten years c) less than five years

7. You have been in your current position for a) less than two
   years b) between two and five years c) more than five years

8. You applied for your current job because a) it seemed ideal for
   you b) you needed a paycheck c) it seemed like it might lead
   somewhere eventually

9. When talking about your company or organization, you use the
   pronoun a) "we" b) "they" c) "it"

10. You daydream about quitting a) sometimes b) often c) rarely,
    if ever

11. Talent is something that a) comes naturally b) you have to
    work hard for c) some people have more than others

12. The most talented people in your workplace **a)** are your closest friends **b)** are a bit self-centered **c)** have the best jobs—go figure!

13. Talent is all about **a)** being efficient **b)** being innovative **c)** networking

14. Having talented people around you makes you feel **a)** competitive **b)** inferior **c)** motivated

15. Your company would do best if it tried to hire people who **a)** had the most ambition **b)** were the most likely to stay **c)** were the most experienced

KEY

1. a) 3 b) 2 c) 1	**6.** a) 1 b) 2 c) 3	**12.** a) 1 b) 3 c) 2
2. a) 2 b) 3 c) 1	**7.** a) 1 b) 2 c) 3	**13.** a) 3 b) 1 c) 2
3. a) 3 b) 2 c) 1	**8.** a) 2 b) 3 c) 1	**14.** a) 2 b) 3 c) 1
4. a) 2 b) 3 c) 1	**9.** a) 1 b) 2 c) 3	**15.** a) 1 b) 3 c) 2
5. a) 3 b) 2 c) 1	**10.** a) 2 b) 3 c) 1	
	11. a) 3 b) 1 c) 2	Total ____

RESULTS

15–22 points

You will CATAPULT TO THE TOP. You have the desire, the ability, and the luck to land in the corner office sooner rather than later. Your ambitions fit well with your current organization, and you would be willing to make all kinds of sacrifices to attain a high position. Expect promotions in the near future, if things remain as they are. Your enthusiasm translates into a friendliness and commitment that everyone appreciates.

23–30 points

You will ADVANCE STEADILY. While you aren't likely to be the youngest head of your organization in history, your solid commitment and work ethic suggest that you will not stagnate for too long in any one position. Furthermore, you seem to be satisfied enough with your work, meaning that you'll likely stick around for a few years. Expect to be offered plenty of opportunities, but be patient.

31–38 points

You will HOLD STEADY. If you stay on the payroll for a while—and you might—it'll be exactly where you are now. Management isn't grooming you to be one of them, and there isn't a natural job up the ladder that makes sense for you to move into. At the same time, you're not so dissatisfied that you will leave the organization in the near future. Expect to tread water for several years before anything changes in a big way.

39–45 points

You will JUMP SHIP. Your current job is not the ideal fit for you, and it is unlikely that you'll hold out long enough to become upwardly mobile. Advancement requires dedication, and it's tough to be dedicated when you're in the wrong environment. You very well might advance rapidly in another organization, or even another field, but you probably won't do so where you are now.

What Do Your Work Clothes Disclose About You?

1. In December, you dress up in holiday clothes a) just before the holidays b) all month long c) not at all

2. For Halloween, you a) wear a costume to work every year b) never wear a costume to work c) wear a costume to work, when it's not too cumbersome

3. For holidays associated with specific colors (such as St. Patrick's Day or Valentine's Day), you a) deliberately don't wear those colors b) wear those colors all over c) wear just a small item with those colors

4. On your birthday, you a) dress up a little b) dress up a lot c) dress normally

5. For days when important things are happening (such as big meetings or interviews), you a) try to look just a little sharper than usual b) try to look really dapper c) try to dress appropriately

6. Among all your coworkers, you are a) one of the best dressed b) dressed OK—you don't keep track of such things, honestly c) not the best or worst dressed

7. When it comes to workplace dress codes, you a) are happy to have a set of rules to help you with your wardrobe b) find them constraining c) usually dress up so much that you don't have to bother reading them

8. When it comes to your coworkers' wardrobes, you pay a) careful attention b) absolutely no attention c) just some attention

9. Dressing well a) can help you climb the ladder b) is fun c) is a pain in the neck, but often necessary

10. Dressing well **a)** makes you feel like part of a professional team **b)** makes you feel like a drone **c)** can be a way to express yourself

11. Suits are **a)** sexy **b)** boring **c)** an easy-enough uniform

12. People who wear things that advertise their company are **a)** distracting **b)** fine, I guess **c)** enthusiastic

13. If an item of clothing has a very small stain, you should **a)** not wear it at all **b)** wear it, but only on slow days **c)** wear it and not worry too much

14. When it comes to casual Fridays, you feel **a)** relieved **b)** annoyed at all the sloppiness **c)** excited

15. Hats at work are **a)** always inappropriate **b)** OK, under certain circumstances **c)** really unusual and cool

KEY

1. a) 2 b) 1 c) 3
2. a) 1 b) 3 c) 2
3. a) 2 b) 1 c) 3
4. a) 2 b) 1 c) 3
5. a) 1 b) 2 c) 3

6. a) 1 b) 2 c) 3
7. a) 3 b) 2 c) 1
8. a) 3 b) 2 c) 1
9. a) 1 b) 2 c) 3
10. a) 3 b) 2 c) 1
11. a) 1 b) 2 c) 3

12. a) 3 b) 2 c) 1
13. a) 3 b) 1 c) 2
14. a) 2 b) 3 c) 1
15. a) 3 b) 1 c) 2

Total ____

RESULTS

15–25 points
You WEAR YOUR HEART ON YOUR SLEEVE. You can't help feeling emotional about workplace fashion, because you can't help feeling emotional in general. When you feel something, it is impossible for you to hide it, so you let it all out right away. Your openness is actually quite healthy, even if it sometimes makes others think that you're too self-centered, or that you draw too much attention to your situation. But you believe that this is far better than being repressed.

26–34 points
You are an INDIVIDUALIST. You think a lot about workplace clothing, but not because you're trying to impress anyone. For you, style is something that each person has to develop independently, and it's often at odds with other people's opinions. You make many of your friends by looking for people who can impress you with how different they are. In this ever-predictable world, it's a noble goal to try to shake things up a little now and then.

35–45 points
You prefer to BLEND IN. You are most comfortable in an environment where many irrelevant choices are made for you in advance—so you like dress codes. External appearances simply don't interest you much, and you see more harm than good in trying to succeed by dressing better than everyone else. In all aspects of life, you are not inclined to make waves. You try to adopt a neutral persona so as not to offend. This is by far the easiest way to avoid being distracted by petty problems.